FAMOUS
FASHION
DESIGNERS

VERSACE

FAMOUS FASHION DESIGNERS

COCO CHANEL

MARC JACOBS

CALVIN KLEIN

RALPH LAUREN

STELLA McCARTNEY

ISAAC MIZRAHI

VALENTINO

VERSACE

FAMOUS FASHION DESIGNERS

VERSACE

Daniel K. Davis

CHELSEA HOUSE
An Infobase Learning Company

VERSACE

Copyright © 2011 by Infobase Learning

Chelsea House
An imprint of Infobase Learning
132 West 31st Street
New York NY 10001

Library of Congress Cataloging-in-Publication Data

Davis, Daniel K.
  Versace / Daniel K. Davis.
    p. cm. — (Famous fashion designers)
  Includes bibliographical references and index.
  ISBN 978-1-60413-980-8 (hardcover)
    1. Versace, Gianni—Juvenile literature. 2. Fashion designers—Italy—Biography—
Juvenile literature. I. Versace, Gianni. II. Title. III. Series.

  TT505.V47D38 2011
  746.9'2092—dc22
  [B   2010034103

Text design and composition by Lina Farinella
Cover design by Alicia Post
Cover printed by Bang Printing, Brainerd, Minn.
Book printed and bound by Bang Printing, Brainerd, Minn.
Date printed: February 2011
Printed in the United States of America

10 9 8 7 6 5 4 3 2 1

Contents

1

A Landmark Show

In some ways, the fashion show that kicked off on July 6, 1997, in Paris was classic Versace: a full house at the Hotel Ritz, loud music, the constant explosion of camera flashes, and, of course, outrageous outfits. The front row was packed, as usual, with Hollywood stars such as Demi Moore, Rupert Everett, Leonardo DiCaprio, actress Kate Capshaw (wife of Steven Spielberg), and Tom Hanks's wife, actress Rita Wilson. Closing out the first day of the show was Gianni Versace's favorite supermodel, Naomi Campbell.

Yet both onstage and behind the scenes, this was quite a different Versace show than in years past. The music, for example, was not the upbeat rock music typical of the events, but rather a mix of what Deborah Ball in her book *House of Versace* calls "hard-driving house music and an eerie, chantlike dirge." With

Departing from his signature style, designer Gianni Versace surprised many with his 1997 autumn-winter collection. The muted colors of his expertly cut suits presented a look that was in direct contrast with the work of newer, more outrageous designers.

the exception of Campbell, the models were not larger-than-life supermodels, but rather mostly young, unknown, thin, pale girls. According to Ball, these models showed the influence of Versace's younger sister, Donatella, with their Goth-style makeup creating "an angry, punched-out look" that matched the dirge-like music.

Even the clothes reflected a new reality in the world of haute-couture fashion. The trend for the past couple of years had been toward minimalism—that is, toward less elaborate creations in favor of more sober, even somber pieces. "About sixty of the eighty pieces were all black," says Ball. "It was Gianni's take on minimalism, with sharp, aggressive tailoring and a brooding air." The show itself was shorter as well—just twenty minutes, or half the length of shows in years past.

There were some throwbacks to Versace's couture heyday, such as the large shoulder pads. "This show was about making the pad not a decoration but a necessity of design in asymmetrical dresses built from one shoulder on the pad itself," Amy Spindler of the *New York Times* (July 9, 1997) reported. Versace told Spindler, "I tried to work on the shoulder, using the pad as the architecture of the dress, to give power and drape with the padding and explore a new shape." But Versace was always known more for looking forward and pushing the boundaries of fashion rather than dwelling in the past.

RIVALS IN REBELLION

Recently, Gianni Versace had some competition in this area of rebelling against conventions, particularly from young designers such as Englishmen Alexander McQueen of the design firm Givenchy and John Galliano of Christian Dior. According to Ball, this new generation "threatened to overshadow Gianni with their wild creativity and onstage antics. The previous season, Gianni's floaty bias-cut gowns seemed downright quaint compared to Galliano's Masai collars and McQueen's gilded bare breasts."

What Is Haute Couture?

Haute couture is the French term for high fashion; literally translated, it means "high dressmaking" or "high sewing." It refers to high-end clothing typically made by hand to the specific measurements of the wearer, as opposed to prêt-à-porter, or ready-to-wear, clothing that is factory made in standardized sizes.

The history of haute couture traces back to English designer Charles Frederick Worth, who worked in Paris in the middle of the nineteenth century. He became famous for using runway models to display his original creations for clients, who would then pick from the designs and have a garment made to their measurements. Though he did not invent the practice of using runway models, "his aggressive self-promotion earned him the titles 'father of haute couture' and 'the first couturier,'" according to essayist Jessa Krick.

For many, haute couture is synonymous with outrageous, elaborate outfits. Yet since its beginnings, it has also meant the best materials, the best craftsmanship, and correspondingly, the highest prices. Amy Spindler wrote in the *New York Times* that no one would question "how the technical outrageousness of Gianni Versace's jeweled, squared-shoulder dresses, Alexander McQueen's jet-beaded jackets or John Galliano's embroidered frock coats and lean skirts might cost $50,000." Though the prices put haute couture beyond the reach of most people, it is still a powerful marketing tool, as a successful haute-couture show can result in great attention to and prestige for a designer's ready-to-wear lines.

At the Paris show, according to Spindler, "Mr. Galliano sees women as sirens, mermaids, muses or princesses, and each piece eloquently projects that vision. No one can doubt he has earned his spot among the great couturiers," while McQueen's show "was in turns so fabulous, so odd, so overwrought, so painstakingly created that it inspired awe as much as fear."

"Up against this," wrote Spindler, "Mr. Versace pushed himself as hard as the younger bucks did." That is not to say, however, that he had abandoned his vision in order to imitate or try to simply outdo his new rivals in outrageousness. Rather, regardless of what others in the industry were doing, Versace was sticking to his vision of stretching himself creatively and expanding what is possible in the world of fashion, while staying true to the craft of clothes making. In distinguishing himself from the young English designers, Versace said, as quoted in *The Versace Legend* by Minnie Gastel, "There are two possible routes [for haute couture]. The hyper-creative English make clothes that are suitable only to be photographed. Others combine imagination and actual exigencies. My way is the second way." In other words, Versace's creations were not just pieces of art, they were meant to be worn.

FREEDOM, INDIVIDUALITY, AND FUN

One of Gianni Versace's driving philosophies was to design clothes for people who wanted to express their freedom and individualism—something they could do only if they could actually wear the clothes. Fashion was a celebration of life, and haute couture was meant to be fun. "Mr. Versace wrote the book on making fashion fun," according to Spindler. "Minimalism and sobriety defined the past five years, but couture is now about having a good time because you can afford to."

In her essay in Versace's book *The Art of Being You*, Ingrid Sischy wrote: "Fun is not only something that Versace encourages, he honors it. He believes in its medicinal powers—just like he believes in the power of creativity." And indeed, after two decades in the fashion industry, Gianni Versace was still having fun. Backstage after the Paris show, Ball writes that he was "thrilled, singing and humming in delight. Wearing black tails over a black polo shirt, he kissed each of the girls."

Unfortunately, the show at the Ritz would be Gianni Versace's last. Just eight days later, he met a tragic end, gunned down by

Eight days after debuting his 1997 autumn-winter collection, Versace was shot and killed in Miami. It was a dramatic loss for the industry, as Versace was one of the most influential figures in fashion.

a serial killer outside his home in Miami. His death shocked the world and left in doubt the fate of one of the most famous houses in fashion. It would be up to his siblings to carry on the family company, and many questioned their ability to do so—especially Donatella's ability to carry on Versace's creativity and vision.

The death could not, however, erase the permanent stamp Gianni Versace had already made on the world of fashion. The couture industry in particular had gone through some soul-searching in the few years leading up to his death, and in *Women's Wear Daily* (*WWD*), Sarah Raper asked the question, "Could haute couture survive? Not long ago it was a hot debate. But the controversy is over, and now, even the most ardent doubters have come to agree—couture is a gold mine. Not in terms of dresses sold—which for most houses is very few—but in terms of publicity and buzz." Gianni Versace recognized this idea of haute couture as a marketing tool to sell his other clothing lines.

He was famous for drawing attention to the Versace brand with his fun, extravagant couture shows, and he and Donatella are credited with inventing the supermodel by paying well-known magazine models to appear in their runways shows, at several times the going rate. Yet at the Paris show, Versace told Raper that back at his shop he also had 40 other outfits for "people who need something else with a sleeve or a different neckline. These clients say to me: 'I'm not Naomi.'" In bringing the same fun and free spirit of his couture shows to his other lines—from eveningwear and daywear to accessories and perfumes—he saved couture while at the same time making the dreams and individuality those outrageous outfits represented accessible to the masses.

Dana Thomas of *Newsweek* quotes Versace as saying, "Even if it took me 20 years, I've got to where I wanted to go." Yet despite all that Gianni Versace had accomplished by the time of the Paris show, he was never one to rest on his laurels. According to Marc Peyser of *Newsweek*, after the Paris show he told Rita Wilson, "Oh, I'm already done with this. I'm already excited about the next thing."

ELEMENTS OF STYLE

When I was young, I wondered, why do men have to dress all the same? Why do they have this boring uniformity? I always liked people who were out of the crowd, who were individuals, who were free, who had a real sense of style, which means their own sense of style. I believe in style. I believe in people who have something to express, who make statements. That's why in the book [Men Without Ties] *there are photos of Picasso and Hemingway and Nijinsky and Cocteau and Robert Mitchum and Nureyev, and for men of today, Elvis, Prince, and Elton. . . .These are people who make statements about their lives via their individual styles of dressing. You can tell the lifestyle of their art, of their living, of their loving. . . .*

Look how many men are wearing sexy underwear these days, with string or lace or stuff like that. Even people who work in ties are wearing lace underwear. It shows how much they need to be free and to express themselves in a different way.

—Gianni Versace, Interview *magazine*

One of the next things was a plan to take the company public with a listing on the stock market. This would provide Versace with the funding needed for him to carry out his grand visions for the future of the brand. In conversation with a friend in April 1997, as quoted by Gastel, Versace showed the same confidence and ambition that had allowed him to achieve so much since launching his own line in 1978. "What I've done in these first twenty years," he said, "is nothing compared to what we're going to do in the next ten."

2

The Versaces
in Calabria

The Versace siblings were all born in Reggio di Calabria (also known as Reggio Calabria, or just Reggio), the oldest, biggest city in the poor and isolated region of Calabria on the toe of Italy, if one pictures the country as a giant boot. The family of their father, Antonio, was from a small nearby farming village. Born in 1915, when the region was still recovering from a devastating earthquake and tsunami in 1908, "Nino," as he was known, grew up to be a semiprofessional soccer player and amateur bicycle racer. Though there were rich members of the extended Versace clan in Italy at the time, Nino's family was poor, and his father had to try to support his family by selling firewood.

The Versace siblings' mother was born Francesca Olandese in 1920 in Reggio. Her father, Giovanni, was a shoemaker by trade and an anti-Fascist anarchist by reputation—a friend of his, a Socialist

Versace's parents, Franca and Nino, raised their family in Reggio, a poor city in southern Italy that is surrounded by water. Young Gianni developed a close relationship with his mother, a talented dressmaker.

politician, was murdered by Fascists in 1924, and the Versaces liked to tell the tale of how local authorities would lock Giovanni up for a couple of days whenever a representative of Italy's Fascist government would visit Reggio.

"Franca," as she preferred to be called, wanted to be a doctor when she grew up, but the backward views about women's role in Calabria at the time prevented her from going to college. According to Deborah Ball in *House of Versace*, Franca's father told her, "You can't go to school with boys. You can't work in a place where there are men. Go learn a trade." She gave up her dream of studying medicine and chose to become a seamstress instead.

Franca managed to get hired on as a trainee by La Parigina, the best seamstress of her day in Reggio. Shortly afterward, she met Nino, who, according to Ball, came into La Parigina's shop to have a garment made by Franca as part of a romantic setup by his sister-in-law. The setup worked, and in 1942, Franca and Nino were married.

THE VERSACE CHILDREN

The first of Nino and Franca's children arrived in November 1943. This was their daughter Fortunata, nicknamed Tinuccia. Their firstborn son, Santo, arrived just over a year later, on December 16, 1944. Two years later, on December 2, 1946, they had another son. They named him Giovanni Maria after Franca's father and Nino's sister, and called him "Gianni."

From when they were very small, Santo took after their father while Gianni had a closer relationship with their mother. Santo was an athlete like his father and later became captain of the Reggio basketball team. Minnie Gastel in *The Versace Legend* quotes Santo as saying that his father "taught me the meaning of work, as a duty first, a right second." Gianni said, "My parents adored Santo because he was the perfect child, the one who studied and always did what he was told," according to Ball. Santo helped his father with his methane gas and coal business, and went on to study business administration and economics at the University of Messina.

Gianni, on the other hand, had little in common with his father other than the opera performances they attended together in Reggio. His father was "a strange man, really, with a very private inner life," Versace told the *New Yorker*'s Andrea Lee. Nino spent much of his time at home by himself, reading poetry. Gianni, for his part, hated helping with his father's business, was not athletic, and did poorly in school. In one famous episode from his youth, one of Gianni's teachers called Franca in to school after she saw some of the sketches of movie actresses he had been drawing in his notebooks when he should have been paying attention in class. To his teacher, there was something perverse about the drawings. "When I was in the fifth grade," he told Michael Neill of *People Weekly*, "my professor called my mother and said, 'Your son is a sex maniac,' and showed her the pictures that I drew, mostly of Sophia Loren and Gina Lollobrigida, wearing evening dresses, with all their curves and big bosoms. My mother said, 'Professor, my son is not a maniac. He just loves fashion and clothes.' I nearly died laughing because at that age, sex was the last thing on my mind. I liked women as a shape to dress."

Oftentimes, Gianni would not go to school at all, but would skip to go to the beach. When he was a bit older, he had someone to join him in his mischief, a partner in crime—a younger sister. In 1953, his older sister, Tinuccia, contracted peritonitis, an inflammation of abdominal wall tissue. Gianni remembers running away from the uncle's house where he and Santo had been sent to stay, returning home only to see his mother kneeling beside Tinuccia in a casket. "Tina has gone to heaven," Franca told Gianni, according to Gastel. "Now I only have you and Santo." She was unable to work for months and wept bitterly. But eventually she grew calmer, and one day told Gianni, "[S]oon you're going to have another little sister." Two years after Tinuccia died, on May 2, 1955, Donatella was born.

Between Franca's dressmaking shop and Nino's new refrigerator- and washing machine-selling business, the family was doing better financially by the time Donatella came along. Add in the fact that she was the baby of the clan, and Donatella grew up in relative comfort. "I was so spoiled," she told Lauren Collins of the *New Yorker*. "I was the best-dressed little girl in my city." She also had a spirit to match her brother Gianni's. They were nine years apart, but they quickly grew very close. According to Susannah Frankel of the *Independent*, Versace once said, "If I was to marry, I would look for a girl like Donatella. Our friendship was from when we were children. We were always together. I can be in China or on the moon; we'll still speak one hundred times a day."

Gastel recounts Gianni recruiting his little sister to help him in his troublemaking, such as warning him of when their parents were approaching so he would not get caught playing when he was supposed to be working, or taking the keys to the family car from their parents' bedside table. "Most children will try to find a way not to obey the orders of an older brother," Donatella said. "But that never happened with us, because everything he asked me to do seemed like fun." When they were a bit older, Gianni would drive them to Calabria's only disco, "with Donatella aged 14, bouncing up and down with excitement on the back seat, wearing go-go boots," wrote Peter Howarth of the *Observer*.

In addition to all these common loves—music, dancing, getting into trouble—Gianni and Donatella also shared their mother's knack for fashion.

FRANCA'S SHOP

Even before she married Nino, Franca had saved enough to open her own shop. She was soon considered the best dressmaker in the region, with a reputation for the same skill and creativity that her son would display years later. "No one was as good as she was," says Gastel. "In the 1950s the fashion that mattered was Paris haute couture, and Italian dressmakers bought paper patterns from Dior, Givenchy and Balenciaga and faithfully reproduced them to make fashionable clothes for their clients. But Franca Versace didn't merely follow the patterns. She was too much her own person to copy from someone else."

Franca's clients were mainly the rich women of the region, "wives of the most prosperous businessmen and professionals of Reggio Calabria. Ladies who would show off their clothes at society parties, extravagant weddings and during the *struscio* when they strolled down the streets of the town center," Gastel writes. However, brides of even less well-to-do families aspired to wear one of Franca's famous wedding gowns. At the wedding itself, more people went to see Franca than the bride, Gianni told the *New Yorker*'s Lee, noting the fantastic hats she would wear for the occasions.

Whether she was creating an evening gown or a wedding dress, one of the reasons for Franca's reputation was her superb skill with her hands. "She was so skilled that she could cut cloth for a new dress without following a pattern, using just pins to mark the edges—a rare ability," says Ball. She also had a strong work ethic, "sometimes working through the night to finish a dress." But perhaps most of all, her clients valued her originality. No matter if she was working from patterns purchased from the couture houses in Rome or taking her inspiration from the hottest designers in Paris, she would add "her own touches, such as a collar of intricately beaded pearls," according to Ball, that made her creations unique.

The Versace children benefited greatly from Franca's talents. They were "among the best dressed in the city," Ball writes. She describes the First Communion outfits Franca made for her children—a ruffled white dress for Tinuccia, white three-piece suits with matching bow ties and gloves for Santo and Gianni—as well as a costume she made for Gianni for the Italian Mardi Gras festival, an extravagant eighteenth-century nobleman costume complete with cape and shoes with large bows. "Gianni," Ball says, "was her best model." For Gianni, Franca's shop would be the perfect classroom for learning his craft.

GIANNI THE APPRENTICE

"[My] most important relationship was with my mother, who was a strong woman," Gianni told Lee. Growing up, Gianni was much closer to his mother than he would ever be to his father, and loved spending time in his mother's shop. There he would take scraps of fabric and make puppets, then put on his own puppet shows. He was something of the shop pet among the seamstresses as well. "I was spoiled by women," he explained to Lee. "I had twenty friends, twenty Mamas. When I came home from school, all the women fussed over me—Giannino, they called me. 'Come with me, Giannino!'"

ELEMENTS OF STYLE

The first dress I can remember, a dress of memory, is a black dress that I recall seeing my mother drape over a client in her dressmaker's shop: Mrs. Ippolito. Over time, this memory has acquired an increasingly precise shape, and that black dress has returned, punctually, in all my collections.

That black dress of my mother, made to be worn with a diamond pin or with a pearl necklace, has from time to time become a dress of neoclassical design, softly draping, or angular and inspired by Picasso's cubist art; very short or long, it has always changed face, taking on an attitude of the moment, an attitude that is very meaningful for our profession.

Today's black dress gives off an energy that is very different from that of many years past. Much time has passed since that dress of memory, but from time to time that black dress has synthesized the rules of fashion, in a short or long version, with asymmetry in the hem or in the neckline, buttoned up or unbuttoned, with anatomical bodice or with irregular pleats, severe and serious or suggestively open behind. This dress will always be a faithful companion in the years to come. Many styles can come and go, but the black dress will remain a must to be reinvented with every new collection, a kind of challenge that is renewed over time.

—*Gianni Versace*, Versace Signatures

He also loved to watch his mother work. He later often recalled hiding behind a red curtain in her shop and observing her in the act of creation, "as if some magic were being performed," Gastel quotes. "I thought: Now my mother's going to shorten the dress in front and leave it longer behind, and then she's going to do something that breaks the rules, something daring. And it would happen, just as I imagined."

His most vivid memory from that time is of a black dress his mother made for Signora Ippolito, one of Franca's upper-class customers. He called it his "dress of memory," and it would influence and inspire him throughout his career.

While he was learning this daringness from his mother, this willingness to break the rules, he was also developing his designer's eye. In an interview with Stephen Schiff of the *New Yorker* magazine, he said, "All the women come in, and first I look at the women. I never look at the clothing she wear. I try to understand the way she move, the way she is, and I try to give advice to her—I was fourteen years old. And these women trusted me. My mother's atelier, it was like a school." "What did you learn there?" Schiff asked. "I learn the way to cut," he said. Getting the cut just right for the client was part of Gianni's focus on quality, something he would become well known for early on. "I like quality," he said in an interview with Gerri Hirshey of *GQ*. "It's important to me—in food, in dress, in people."

After attending a technical high school in Reggio, he went to work for his mother full-time in 1966, continuing his education in Franca's shop. He credits his mother's wealthy clientele with furthering that education. "You live in an ambiance where rich people come to buy, you learn. I was always demanding," he said to Hirshey.

The rich ladies trusted him, and wanted him to pick out the materials for their dresses. This would become one of his primary duties. In his book *Versace Signatures*, Versace describes the trips he took to buy materials for his mother: "I shuttle back and forth between Reggio and Messina, I took the ferry, and each time I tried to choose more beautiful and extraordinary materials. With the remaining money I bought an enormous ice cream and on the way home looked forward to the pleasure of astonishing my mother with my choices." He would later make trips to Paris and London, gaining even more exposure to the possibilities of the fashion world.

Gianni Versace was influenced by the people, landscape, and designs of his homeland. Around the time he began working for his mother, Italian fashion was very colorful and splashy.

Yet he would always look back to his Calabrian youth as a time of great inspiration. According to James Servin of the *New York Times*, "Interestingly, Mr. Versace has named as two early influences his mother . . . and the prostitutes who lived down the street. Today, his is still a world of contrasts, a Milan-based empire built on family ties and worldly flash."

He also drew from the landscape and culture of Calabria itself. He told Amy Spindler of the *New York Times*, "When you are born in a place such as Calabria and there is beauty all around—a Roman bath, a Greek remain—you cannot help but be influenced by the classical past." Spindler went on, "Those themes, the Italian Baroque, Grecian motifs and Etruscan symbols, were woven into his collections." They are themes he took with him when he left Calabria first for Tuscany, then for the up-and-coming fashion center of Milan, Italy.

ON HIS OWN

In 1965, when Gianni Versace was 18 years old, Franca opened her first Elle di Franca Versace boutique next to her atelier, or design workshop. Versace was put in charge of traveling to buy clothes for the store, first to the Palazzo Pitti in Florence, Italy, and later to Paris and London. His choices were influenced by his clients back home. He learned what the younger women who came into the store wanted, fashions that they could not find elsewhere in Reggio. He also learned how to make each woman look her best and "stand out, such as tying a scarf around her waist or fastening a shawl of fluttering voile at her neck with a jeweled brooch," Ball writes. "He learned how women saw themselves and how to make them feel attractive."

He then put that learning to practice in creating his own designs. On one of his trips to the Palazzo Pitti in 1972, those designs and his insight into what appealed to young shoppers impressed textile manufacturers Ezio Nicosia and Salvatore Chiodini, owners of the knitwear house Florentine Flowers in the town of Lucca in Tuscany. When they offered him a contract to design a clothing collection, he called his friend and star designer Walter Albini and asked how much he got. He then asked Nicosia and Chiodini for the same amount—4 million lire—and somewhat to Versace's surprise, they agreed. Gianni Versace, 25 years old, said good-bye to his beloved mother and the rest of his family and moved to Tuscany.

In his very first designing job, he already showed inventiveness and a willingness to take risks. "Although he knew virtually nothing about knitwear," Gastel writes, "he had a very clear idea of how he wanted the collection to look, with lavish, complicated patterns, things like cables and stitches on the bias, that had never been done before. Since he didn't know anything about the technical specifications for knitted fabrics, he simply treated the material as if it were woven."

Nicosia and Chiodini gave him free reign to experiment and design as he saw fit, and it paid off—the spring-summer collection turned out to be a big hit. Fresh off of this success, Versace set his

The Rise of Milan

Milan is in the far north of Italy, almost as far from Reggio di Calabria as New York is from Chicago. In the early 1960s, Milan was not yet the fashion powerhouse it would be a few years later—Paris was the undisputed capital of the fashion world at the time—but that would soon change.

For centuries Italy had been known for its excellent yet relatively inexpensive fabrics. After World War II, the prices for couture fashions from Paris rose dramatically, leading more Italians to turn to Rome for their couture. Giovanni Giorgini, one of the leading Italian buyers for American department stores, gave the Italian designers a showcase for their lines first at his home in Florence and then at the Palazzo Pitti.

In the early 1970s, avant-garde designers, such as Walter Albini and Rosita and Ottavio Missoni, moved to Milan to take advantage of the benefits of its various ad agencies and its proximity to Italy's textile producers. This in turn attracted Gianni Versace and other new designers. Together these designers would soon establish Milan as a center of the fashion universe.

sights higher. Milan was the rising star in the fashion world at the time, and he knew this was where he wanted to be.

Just months after he moved to Tuscany, Versace uprooted himself again and moved to Milan. There he received an offer from fashion businessman Gigi Monti to create a collection for the company he co-owned, FTM. Versace fell in with other young designers and models in Milan and continued to attract the attention of design firms. When the Callaghan Group in Novara, Italy, near Milan, looked for someone to replace their recently departed in-house designer Albini, Versace got the call. He was on his way.

3

Rocking the
Fashion World

When Gianni Versace took over for Walter Albini designing for the Callaghan Group, he had big shoes to fill. It did not take him long to fill them. In the book *The Versace Legend*, Callaghan founder Marisa Zanetti Greppi told author Minnie Gastel that while Versace originally had to follow Albini's style closely to match their clients' expectations, he eventually found a style all his own. "He became more confident, he began to express himself," Greppi said. "The real Versace appeared, and he was a triumph."

Versace soon branched out from Callaghan. Even as he continued to design for that firm, he worked for a brief stint at Alma in Barregio, also right outside of Milan, and then signed a contract with the clothing company Genny. At Genny, his job was to make the company's clothes more appealing to the younger generation.

At both Callaghan and Genny, Versace had already begun the creative mixing and matching for which he would become famous as his career developed. "The fact is, Gianni revolutionized fashion," according to Greppi. "Before him, clothes were sober, bourgeois, often boring. Gianni added color, he began to mix his fabrics and use unusual materials." Ball says. "At Genny, Gianni displayed the first flashes of inspiration that would later become his signature look. He was a man of mixtures, combining masculine with feminine, sportswear with dressier items, leather with silk—and thus breaking long-standing rules of fashion."

With this, he was on his way to finding his own true style, while at the same time finding audiences among both shoppers and the press. He was featured in a spread in Italian *Vogue* in 1975 and received praise for his Rustica collection for Callaghan in French *Vogue* in 1976. The Callaghan lines sold well, and Genny's sales tripled from 1973 to 1980.

In 1977, he had his first American show, for the new Complice line (started by Genny founders Arnaldo and Donatella Complice) at Studio 54 in New York, and it was a big hit. Diana Vreeland, the legendary former editor of *Vogue* magazine, was on hand. "I knew all about her, admired her, dreamed of meeting her, and now for my first show in America she was there, watching me with interest and tenderness," he wrote in *Versace: Signatures*. "At the end she hugged me and said, 'I have never seen anyone drape a dress so well and in such little time.' No one could have given me a greater compliment, and it remained in my heart."

It was during this period that Versace believed he finally did find his own style. In *Interview* magazine, he told Hal Rubenstein, "I think the first time I sensed the key to my style was in 1976, when I did a collection combining lots of leather with silk. No one had shown an entire collection in leather or other hard materials before, with the desired effect being elegance and class. When it became a kind of revolution, I realized that putting together the past with the future, tradition with the avant-garde, was the key to modern fashion."

Franca Versace's enormous success as a dressmaker influenced Gianni, who, in turn, reached out to his siblings for help with his growing fashion business. The family further expanded with Donatella's children and Santo's family (*above*).

That creative mixing was not the only defining characteristic that Versace showed in those early days of his career. Even when he was designing for other people, Gianni Versace displayed the tireless work ethic for which he would later become known. "He was a workhorse, a flood of inspiration," Greppi told Gastel. "He arrived in the office, took off his jacket and rolled up his sleeves." Inspiration for a design idea could strike him at any time, so he always had a notebook handy in which he could sketch his ideas, even if they occurred to him in the middle of the night. Before runway shows, he'd stay up until three or four in the morning making last-minute changes, then during the show, he would stay backstage to help dress the models himself.

While Versace was designing for Callaghan, Genny, and Complice, his sister, Donatella, was studying literature and languages at the University of Florence. "My mother didn't want me to be in fashion," she told Susannah Frankel of the *Independent*. "She was in the fashion business, so was my brother, and she thought it was too crazy for me. She wanted me to be married with children, to be independent, yes, but not to have a crazy life." Despite this, Donatella traveled on weekends up to Milan to help out. The little sister on whom he used to try out design ideas back in Calabria was now helping him in the studio. According to Cathy Horyn of *Vanity Fair*, "the funny thing about that is, Gianni never was inspired by her looks. It was her truthfulness he liked—and the way she could sum up something in about a fourth of a second."

Versace would get some assistance from his big brother as well. By 1976, Santo had joined his younger brother in Milan, first on a part-time basis to help with strategy and negotiating contracts, and later full-time to run the business. He had graduated from the University of Messina, where he studied business administration and economics, and this education and know-how would be crucial to Gianni Versace as he embarked upon the next phase of his career: launching his own fashion line.

DESIGNING FOR HIMSELF

Gianni Versace became an accomplished and sought-after designer creating lines for Callaghan, Genny, and Complice, but, as Lowri Turner writes in *Gianni Versace: Fashion's Last Emperor*: "Santo realized from the start that control was the key to success." Santo wrote in the brochure for the Versus launch in 1989: "To begin with, Versace decided to stay independent, becoming one of the few major labels in control of the entire fashion cycle, from design to retailing." This independence actually started before Gianni Versace even began designing for a "Versace" brand.

In 1977, under Santo's guidance, his brother started the company Gianni Versace S.r.L. The company's logo was the head of Medusa, the Greek mythological monster who turned anyone who looked at her to stone. The inspiration for the logo came from a mosaic floor in Roman ruins that the Versace siblings used to play in as children. Medusa's head was a fitting symbol for his company, Gastel quotes Gianni Versace as saying, because "those who fall in love with the Medusa have no way back. So why not imagine that those whom Versace conquers—that they, too, cannot go back?"

Then in 1978, in partnership with boutique owner Giovina Moretti, the brothers found a showroom and store on the most desirable shopping street in Milan, Via della Spiga. When the store opened, however, they had no Versace line to sell, so instead they sold some of Gianni Versace's creations from the Genny, Callaghan, and Complice lines.

Gianni Versace's first line under the Versace name would soon follow. On March 28, 1978, he made his debut with a small collection for women at the Palazzo della Permanente in Milan. It was a chaotic show behind the scenes, according to Ball, with models doing their own makeup, Donatella and some of her friends helping the models get dressed, and Versace making last-second adjustments.

Things on the runway were not much better. Ball writes: "[T]he girls bumped into one another on the crowded runway, twirling willy-nilly and tapping their toes distractedly to the blaring disco music. . . . But despite all his effort, the press largely hated the collection, finding the clothes gimmicky and confused. Privately, Gianni had to agree that it wasn't his best work."

Gianni Versace's mother, Franca, was in attendance for the opening of the Versace shop on Via della Spiga, but traveling had become more difficult for her during the years since she fell ill with cirrhosis of the liver following an operation in 1965. Then, on

June 27, 1978, Franca Versace succumbed to her disease and died at a clinic in Modena, Italy. She was 58 years old. Donatella was just weeks away from graduating from the University of Florence at the time. She rushed to the clinic to be by her mother's side, but arrived too late. She never went back to Florence. Instead, she joined Versace in Milan and moved into his apartment. "The loss of Franca had shaken both of them deeply and brought them even closer," writes Ball. "Over the next few years, they happily spent virtually every waking hour together."

Donatella was by her brother's side for his first full collection, in March 1979, again at the Palazzo della Permanente. Unfortunately, more bad reviews followed as his audience grew confused about his switch from the fresh, modern ideas of his past designs to this show's more traditional, conventional creations. According to Gastel, "Versace himself later said this collection was one that least represented him. And the Italian fashion journalists were fairly cool." One good thing that came out of that show, however, was meeting a young American model named Paul Beck. Versace used Paul in some more runway shows and even an early ad campaign. Ball says that Paul "became a fixture among Gianni's group of friends. Soon, he was practically living at Gianni's apartment on Via Melegari." While he did not model for Versace for long, he would later play a much bigger role in the Gianni Versace story.

Versace started another important relationship in 1979 as well. Richard Avedon was one of the most successful and respected photographers of his time. He was expensive, but his work style was just what Versace sought for his advertising campaigns. "They were like brothers, they had the same take on things, the same drive for perfection and the same energy," Donatella told Luisa Zargani of *WWD*. The results were what Versace was looking for as well, with the press praising their first ad campaign, for the spring-summer 1980 beachwear line. Avedon enjoyed working for Versace as well. According to Gastel, Avedon once told an interviewer that Gianni Versace "has a big heart, and great love and respect for art and artists. It's rare; he's special. If you photograph for Revlon or Chanel or Ralph Lauren, it's work. . . . With Versace, it's different." He would end up working for the House of Versace for almost 18 years.

Gianni Versace's clothes started to click with the press as well. For the spring-summer 1980 season, with the debut of his "Optical" style, Versace won glowing reviews for his creativity and his linking of modern ideas to the past—part of what he called the "key to his style" that he discovered in 1976.

As the 1970s drew to a close, Gianni Versace had already left his mark on the world of fashion. In the August 1979 issue of *GQ*, Peter Carlsen wrote: "Perhaps he's the strongest reason why the Italians have seized the initiative in men's fashion innovation from the French."

Versace told Carlsen that his fall collection "embodies everything I've learned about clothes and life up through the present. It's

---

ELEMENTS OF STYLE

During the seventies I began to transfer my restlessness, seeking to find ways of combining different forms and materials in ways that had never been tried. It was during that period that the first contrasts appeared in my fashions, later becoming the key to all my creations. That reference to the past mixed with the present, that antithesis in the pairing of furs and silk, which came to me spontaneously in those years, expressed the desire for a double vision in all things: an elegant and traditional face and an avant-garde face, the face of the past and that of the future. Gold became mixed with jute, simple cottons with those rich or with silk.

The year 1979 saw the birth of my disciplined masculine negligence, *which followed no rules at all.*

—*Gianni Versace,* Versace Signatures

also a kind of farewell to this phase of my life. My next collection will be completely different."

He felt confident enough at this time to stop designing for Complice. This allowed him to focus more attention on the Versace line, though he also kept designing for Callaghan and Genny. His clothes had become more daring by this point, taking influence from the London punk scene as well as *Star Wars*. He was also doing well financially—his company recorded $15 million in sales in its first year—to the point that in 1980 he was able to buy and restore Villa Fontanelle, a mansion built in 1865 on the shore of Lake Como. It was a fitting start to the extravagant 1980s, a decade for which Gianni Versace would create some of the defining fashions.

AN ESTABLISHED STAR

The 1980s proved to be a decade of great growth for Gianni Versace, but he was not alone in his success. "This was the decade of the *look*," writes Turner. "It was a golden moment for Italian fashion; between 1971 and 1981, the number of clothing shops doubled and employment in the sector grew rapidly. People wanted status symbols to show for their money, their success, their well-being. And sporting a label was the simplest way to announce one had arrived. The designers became stars. The champions of Italian Style, [Giorgio] Armani and Versace, divided the territory."

Donatella started off the decade by becoming the stylist for the company's advertising campaigns in addition to doing the models' hair and makeup for runway shows. She also started being called Versace's "muse" by the press because of the opinions she gave her brother on his work. "He sought her views on every aspect of his designs, from color schemes to dress choices for the runway," writes Ball. In another unofficial role, she was the more social of the two, going out late at night to dance and have fun—more and more often with Paul Beck, whom Versace hired to work on accessories—while he retired after a long day's work. This helped Donatella stay on top of the latest trends among young people and

Oroton

Gianni Versace drew inspiration from medieval warriors' coats of chain mail when, in his men's autumn-winter 1982–1983 collection, he showed clothes featuring inserts of mesh made from interlinking metal rings. The material was too heavy and did not drape right for women's wear, so Versace went back to the drawing board, this time with the help of a German craftsman.

The result was Oroton, a mesh made of metal disks that do not interlink, but rather, as Chiara Buss writes in *The Art and Craft of Gianni Versace*, "serve to join a series of solid discs at four points." The material behaved more like silk than metal, giving it the versatility Versace sought. "It clings to the body," writes Buss, "and can be draped, dyed or patterned."

Oroton was an immediate sensation. Versace never tired of the material, using it in every collection from then on. His last runway show ended with Naomi Campbell wearing an Oroton bridal gown. "The invention of Oroton constituted one of the most important advances in the field of postwar haute couture," according to Buss. It cemented Versace's reputation and was, writes Lowri Turner, "(q)uite simply . . . one of the sexiest fabrics ever to hit a catwalk."

came in handy as she developed relations with rock stars, movie stars, and other celebrities.

Santo contributed to the House of Versace's success during this time, too, setting strategy and handling sales while his brother and Donatella concentrated on the creative side of the business. He also foresaw a real estate boom in Milan, so the siblings took some of the company's profits to buy a huge palazzo on Via Gesú in 1981. This space would eventually hold the headquarters of Versace S.r.L. as well as a private apartment for Gianni Versace.

With both his new work space and his reputation as an elite designer secured, Versace was set to embark on a string of successes, accolades, collaborations, and partnerships through the rest of the 1980s. The year 1982 was a particularly important one on both a personal and professional level. In that year, he launched a new Versace perfume and gave several successful shows in the United States. He also introduced Oroton, the metal-mesh material he invented with the help of a German craftsman. The Oroton collection won Gianni Versace the L'Occhio d'Oro award for the best fashion designer of the season, the first of four times he would win the award in his career.

Santo and his girlfriend Cristiana's first child, their daughter Francesca, was born in 1982, and Donatella and Paul announced their engagement that year as well. Donatella and Paul got married on the first day of spring in 1983, and Santo and Cristiana the following year.

The year 1982 also saw Versace designing costumes for the theater for the first time, in this case for the Richard Strauss ballet *Josephs Legende* at the La Scala opera house in Milan. More importantly, it was at the La Scala debut that Versace met Antonio D'Amico, the love of his life. Antonio was just 24 years old to Versace's 36, and Versace was dating another man at the time, but there was an instant connection. Versace asked Antonio to sit at his table at dinner after the ballet, then asked for his phone number at the end of the evening.

Like Gianni Versace, Antonio was born in Italy's deep south, though he grew up in Milan. Antonio's mother was also a seamstress. Yet it was more their differences that made them a good couple, according to Ball. "Gianni, full of restless energy and brio, worked constantly, while Antonio, more even-tempered, was his anchor.... Gianni found that Antonio's modest background, earthy wit, and forthright manner grounded him at a time when Gianni was being swept up in the whirlwind of his growing success." The two started spending more and more time

Versace found love in 1982 with Antonio D'Amico. Their relationship would last more than 15 years. *Above,* D'Amico attends a memorial for Versace in Milan.

together, and Versace soon found ways of bringing Antonio into the family business. Though Donatella never warmed to Antonio, he and Versace stayed by each other's side over the next 15 years, through good times and bad, and Antonio would be one of the first on the scene when Versace died.

Meanwhile, Gianni Versace continued to roll up one success after another. He became more experimental with materials and techniques, leading to rave reviews. The *Daily News Record* wrote: "Gianni Versace has taken a quantum leap into the future, exploring new materials and industrial technologies in his fall 1983 men's wear. This is Versace's most independent and avant-garde collection to date." He won the prestigious Cutty Sark award for men's fashion in the United States in 1983, and he was the subject of exhibits in Verona, Italy, and Munich, Germany. In 1984, he won his second L'Occhio d'Oro award.

He designed for La Scala again in 1984 as well, this time for *Dionysos* with choreography by Maurice Béjart. Versace collaborated with Béjart many more times over the years, and said of the choreographer, "I feel I am his ideal disciple. He has taught me what theater means: to dare the undareable, to put everything in question," according to Gastel.

It was around this time that the Versaces started cultivating their more mainstream celebrity relationships as well. In 1985, Versace lent his Lake Como house to newlyweds Bruce Springsteen and Julianne Phillips for their honeymoon. Versace outfits appeared on Michael Jackson and Paul McCartney in their video for "Say, Say, Say" and on John Taylor in Duran Duran's "View to a Kill" video. The TV show *Miami Vice* featured some Versace clothes, and Don Johnson, the star of the show, frequented the Miami Versace boutique. "We have to shut the door and lock it when he's inside," store owner Melissa Gottlieb told Michael Neill of *People Weekly*. "Whatever Don Johnson buys becomes a bestseller, so I get upset if we don't have a lot in stock."

When designing a new collection, Versace was fearless; he used nontraditional materials and drew inspiration from unlikely sources, such as medieval armor. Fashion critics raved over his work, but he continued to challenge himself with new goals. Not long after receiving his second L'Occio d'Oro award for best designer (*above*), Versace released his own haute couture line and began to make an impression on Hollywood stars.

In 1986—the year that Cristiana gave birth to her and Santo's son, Daniel, and Donatella and Paul welcomed their daughter, Allegra, into the world—Versace met Elton John when the rock star stopped by the Versace boutique in Milan. Versace closed the store for the afternoon so he, Antonio, and Paul could help Elton shop. The two struck up a friendship immediately, one that lasted the rest of Versace's life and also resulted in a strong friendship between Elton and Donatella. Donatella even named her son Daniel, born in 1990, after the Elton John song, according to Ball.

That same year, Gianni Versace received the decoration of Commendatore della Repubblica Italiana from the president of Italy, and his creations were the subject of a fashion photography exhibit at the Musée de la Mode et du Costume in Paris. As part of the ceremonies for the Paris show, he received a special medal from Paris mayor Jacques Chirac.

BREAKING IN TO HAUTE COUTURE

Another Béjart collaboration followed in 1986, for a production of the ballet *Malraux ou La metamorphose des dieux* in Brussels, Belgium. Versace took inspiration from haute couture for his costumes, and his theater work started influencing his other designs as well. Gastel quotes the fashion historians Nicoletta Bocca and Chiara Buss as saying that "he took what he had learned from his studies for the costumes and he applied it to some of the clothes in his collections.... With the costumes for *Malraux* Versace moved toward a fresh encounter with French couture of the twenties and thirties, a move that would deeply influence the development of his fashion and of the Versace Couture line." Though he had not yet tried his hand at a full haute-couture line at that point, his first attempt was not far off.

Then, Versace took the next step in his career. "Gianni Versace to present first couture collection," read the headline in the December 2, 1988, issue of *WWD*. Even though haute couture had been almost exclusively the realm of French designers up to that point, the time was right for Versace to make such a move. He was riding high on the string of awards and successes that had made him an established star in the fashion world. He had also been building up to his first haute-couture collection, not only with the costumes for ballets but with custom-made creations for celebrities and socialites as well.

Still, the move was a bold one. "He was a rich, successful man when he decided to design couture for the first time," wrote Amy Spindler in the *New York Times*. "Only love of his craft could make a designer undertake such a risk as couture, when he had no need of the publicity and the risk might never yield rewards."

Ball, however, provides additional motivation for the move into haute couture: the growing rivalry between Gianni Versace and Giorgio Armani. Armani was at that point the designer to the stars. "The 1990 Oscars were an Armani fashion show," Ball writes. "He dressed Michelle Pfeiffer, Jodie Foster, Julia Roberts, and Jessica Lange, as well as six leading men, including Denzel Washington." Versace's new haute-couture line would help him land more celebrities, and more celebrities wearing Versace clothes would lead to more prestige—and in turn more sales—for his other clothing lines.

Gianni Versace called the new haute-couture line Atelier Versace and set the debut for January 25, 1989, at the Musée d'Orsay in Paris. The debut was not a full collection, however, but what Versace called a "concept." Nor was it a runway show, but rather a dinner for 250 people. And he did not use professional models to show off the fashions, but instead had friends who had already ordered the clothes serve as models. The first full haute couture runway show was still a year off.

During that year, Versace remained busy, as did his siblings. The Versus line, launched in July 1989 with a menswear line, was followed by a women's collection in October. With its target audience of younger consumers, it was a perfect project for Donatella to work on. "Exactly how much of a free hand Donatella was given with Versus by Gianni is a matter of some debate," writes Turner. "The exuberance of the range—low on simple white toga dresses and high on scarlet leather—suggests that it was (and still is) Donatella's baby."

Then came the time for the first full runway show for Atelier Versace, at the Ritz Hotel in Paris. Versace presented what Bernadine Morris of the *New York Times* called a "short, sexy, glittery collection" at the hotel's pool area, which he rented for $40,000 and spent hundreds of thousands of dollars more to fix up for the show.

The show itself was a stunner. "If you like to walk on the wilder side of rock (or the Sunset Strip), Versace makes couture just for you," wrote *WWD*. "His collection Saturday night at the Ritz had more feathers, pearls, rhinestones, jewels, tassels, beading and embroidery than Paris has seen in some time. He even put jewels and tassels on his shoes, proving once and for all that if anyone deserves the title of Cecil B. De Mille of fashion, Gianni does."

The actress Julie Andrews, wearing a Versace outfit, called the collection "a tour de force." "Veterans would agree with her," Morris wrote. When the 45-minute show was over and Gianni Versace appeared, the crowd burst into thunderous applause.

Versace and Donatella stayed at their postshow party until 10:00 P.M. and then had a late dinner at the Ritz Grille, basking in the success of the first Versace haute-couture show.

4

High Fashion

The connection between Gianni Versace's work for the theater, his haute-couture designs, and his ready-to-wear lines was instantly apparent to the fashion press. Bernadine Morris of the *New York Times* said, "[T]he line of demarcation between Versace's designs for the stage and the clothes he sells in 120 shops around the world is not too strict.... His clothes for the theater add wonder and excitement to his semiannual fashion shows, and often the ideas spill over into his regular collection." Versace himself provided an excellent example: "I was among the first designers to do tights," he said to Morris. "That's because I designed for the ballet so much and the dancers have to move. So very often, tights were the basis for the elaborate skirts and shawls that the character wore. And they were often embroidered and jeweled, like jump suits often are today."

When Richard Strauss's *Capriccio* opened at the Royal Opera in London in 1991 featuring Versace costumes, "[t]he sellout crowd gasped and applauded as the sumptuously clothed cast appeared," according to Susan Heller Anderson of the *New York Times*. Recognizing the impact that these costumes could have, when the new Versace store opened on Madison Avenue in New York City, Versace dressed mannequins in ballet, opera, and theater costumes he had designed since 1984.

Versace was also getting more successful at landing big-name celebrities to wear his clothes. By June 1991, he was already the designer of choice for rock stars such as Bruce Springsteen, Eric Clapton, Sting, and George Michael when the King of Pop, Michael Jackson, chose to wear Versace clothes for his new video and album cover. Soon after, Versace landed one of the only people at the time who could rival Michael Jackson for star power: Diana, Princess of Wales. She was in the midst of separating from Prince Charles and looking for a new image when she appeared in the British edition of *Harper's Bazaar* in a now famous blue-silk couture dress. Deborah Ball in *House of Versace* writes, "The pictures showing a relaxed, sexy Diana, shorn of jewelry and wearing the sleek gown, were an instant hit—for her and for the gown's designer."

During this same period—in which he won two more L'Occhio d'Oros, in 1990 and 1991—Versace reached another level in his designs as well. Although his elaborate creations and bright colors helped define fashion in the 1980s, particularly the *Miami Vice* years, it was "principally in the key 1991–93 period," says Lowri Turner in *Gianni Versace: Fashion's Last Emperor*, that the "quintessential Versace look was forged." In December 1991, Wood Hochswender of the *New York Times* wrote: "Versace has evolved into a designer with a signature look, based on a mix of tailored clothes and prints, which typically mix classical and modern images: the lyre, a Roman vase, men in athletic tights, red dragons, blue serpents, black-and-white checks. As put together by countless regular women, they form a recognizable and modern ensemble:

a dark, trim jacket, a matching or slightly contrasting skirt and a stained-glass blouse underneath."

It was also during this time that he made another of his lasting impacts on the industry. "To watch a Versace catwalk show in the early 1990s was to witness a parade of colour and sparkle, the like of which would have made a Las Vegas showgirl blush. . . . It was an assault on the senses," writes Turner. Versace runway shows had long featured loud music and bright lights, but in the early 1990s, another element appeared: the supermodel. Up to that point, there

The Elizabeth Hurley Dress

Perhaps the most famous and notorious of Versace's scanty dresses made a big splash when it hit magazine pages around the world in 1994. At the time, Elizabeth Hurley was a 29-year-old model known only as the girlfriend of actor Hugh Grant. When she appeared with Grant on the red carpet for the London premiere of his movie *Four Weddings and a Funeral* in a Versace creation, however, she became an overnight sensation. The dress was a punk-inspired black slit gown with large gold safety pins just barely containing Hurley's curvy figure. The dress is largely credited with launching her acting career.

At a Gianni Versace exhibition at London's Victoria and Albert Museum in 2002, the dress was one of two (along with the Princess Diana powder-blue couture dress) that greeted people upon entry. In 2008, the U.K. department store Debenhams conducted a poll in which the Hurley safety-pin dress was voted the greatest red carpet gown of all time. A Debenhams's spokesperson said, "Liz Hurley's daring safety pin dress is one of the most famous black dresses worn on the red carpet, which made her a household name overnight. Our research shows how iconic the dresses worn on the red carpet have become with many of the stars making headlines from their outfits."

were generally two categories of fashion models: one for photography, one for runway shows. "They never trod on each other's turf," according to Joshua Levine of *Forbes*. "Runway models walk better, are generally thinner, and get about $2,000 a show."

Versace and Donatella were less interested in the way the models walked, however, than in other ways they could help sell not only their non-couture clothing lines but their expanding offering of bags, watches, and other accessories. So they paid some of the world's top fashion photography models up to $10,000 or even $15,000 each to appear in a single show. In doing so, they helped turn models such as Cindy Crawford, Naomi Campbell, Linda Evangelista, Claudia Schiffer, and Christy Turlington into celebrities themselves. But more importantly, it got Versace the press he and Donatella sought. "Maybe some of them didn't walk too well," writes Turner, "but their faces were pure magic in the long lenses. . . . With Claudia, Christy, Cindy, et al., every picture was a *Vogue* cover." And every couture outfit on a *Vogue* cover had the potential to translate into increased sales for all Versace-branded products.

VISIONARY OR VULGAR?

Gianni Versace's runway shows were monuments to excess, and that in part carried over into his personal life as well. In 1991, he and Antonio made a stopover to visit Donatella in Miami on their way to Cuba. They hired a driver to show them around town, and he brought them to Miami's South Beach district. "I [fell] in love with the spirit of the city. . . . There are no rules," Versace told Charles Gandee of *Vogue*. The next year, Versace paid $2.95 million for Casa Casuarina, an apartment building then known as the Amsterdam Palace, on Ocean Drive in one of Miami's most expensive neighborhoods, where Madonna and Sylvester Stallone also had houses. The 13,356-square-foot (1,240-square-meter) building, built in 1930, was historic but in bad shape. The next year, he bought the vacant Revere Hotel next door for $3.7 million, only to demolish it in order to build a pool and a guesthouse as part of a renovation of the entire property that cost many millions more.

Miami soon influenced Versace's designs, according to Gandee, inspiring his spring 1993 ready-to-wear collection, "which featured the kind of blinding colors, flamboyant prints, and somewhat unsettling libidinal energy that Miami's Latin and gay communities like to flaunt."

This "flaunting" and excess both in his personal life and in his designs made Gianni Versace a target of critics in the fashion world and beyond. Their favorite buzzword to apply to him and/or his fashions was "vulgar." For conservative critics, his close ties to the decadent world of rock and roll only fueled these notions. The criticisms leveled at him reached a peak following his "bondage" collection presented in March 1992 in Milan. Versace described the collection as having three themes: "The aristocrat cowboy meets baroque, a homage to American designer Charles James and an updating of wardrobe basics like jeans and trenches with a fun bit of sado-masochism." Reviewing the collection for the *New York Times*, Bernadine Morris said it had a "disturbing undertone" and claimed that, "[a]t a time when it is hard for fashion to shock, these leather tops managed."

Many people found the collection offensive, including fashion critic Holly Brubach of the *New Yorker*. "There were people who loved it, who thought it was brilliant, the greatest thing he had ever done. And others of us, mostly women, could barely evaluate the design aspect of it because we were so offended," she told James Servin of the *New York Times*. "I have to say that I hated it."

"I understand if these straps of leather are not to everyone's liking," Versace countered. "I don't mind if people say I'm vulgar." Later he rejected the charges of vulgarity outright, telling Italian TV channel RAI UNO, "Vulgarity doesn't exist. It's an attitude. Stupidity is vulgar. But a woman who dresses badly but is intelligent and happy to be the way she is, is not vulgar. Vulgarity is for people who are frightened, not for us. I believe I've done [women] good

In 1994, Elizabeth Hurley wore a form-fitting black Versace dress that seemed to be held together with gold safety pins. The daring frock instantly made Versace a household name and is credited with starting Hurley's acting career. *Above,* Donatella Versace poses in front of the safety-pin dress in London's Victoria and Albert Museum.

without subjugating anyone because the woman decides whether to wear Chanel or Versace clothes. There is always a democratic choice at the root." Individuality and freedom are what mattered most to Versace. "Whether it's chic or vulgar is besides the point," he said to *Architectural Digest*'s Gini Alhadeff. He was talking about home design, but added, "It's the same for women. I'd take a gaudy funny woman over a boring elegant one any day."

When New York's Fashion Institute of Technology held its Gianni Versace: Signatures exhibition in November 1992, the largest design exhibition ever for the institute, bondage pieces were featured prominently among the more than 150 designs on display. Yet despite the publicity those pieces garnered for Versace, it was the theater costumes that generated the most excitement at the show, both for fans and for Versace himself. "I'm really excited to show these costumes—it is the first time in America for a lot of them because many of the productions were never staged here," he told Elizabeth Barr of the *Daily News Record*. He did not deny his role as the king of rock-and-roll fashion, but as he said to Kathleen Beckett of *Harper's Bazaar*, there is also "opera star, museum director, actress, painter. Maybe they don't make headlines, but they come to Como. . . . I think [designing for the theater] is the best thing I do. I'm really proud of that work."

THE RISE OF DONATELLA

The irony of the charges of vulgarity is that while many of them were fueled by the idea of Gianni Versace being linked to the worlds of sex, drugs, rock and roll, and homosexuality, he, in fact, lived a very quiet life outside of work. He did not do drugs or get drunk, and was known for retiring to his house by 11:00 P.M. after a long day at the atelier. "People think I'm all about sex, disco and rock," he told Alhadeff, "but I like a quiet life; I'm in love with houses."

Of the Versace siblings, Donatella was the one that led the rock-and-roll lifestyle, hosting parties and staying out dancing late into the night. Part of this was in her efforts to court as many high-profile celebrities as possible to wear Versace clothing, and part of it was what she saw as her role in life. "I always thought I was born to cheer up everybody," she told David Furnish in *Interview* magazine.

Her responsibilities within the company grew during the 1990s as well. Up to this point, she had been known primarily as Versace's muse, providing important opinions or taking his ideas and making them modern. "I push Gianni forward," she told Constance White of the *New York Times*. "I try not to make him fall in love with what he did last season. We can't be too safe, because that's not what fashion is about." Donatella was more in touch with the latest trends, so he listened to her advice. "If my sister wants to do something, okay," he said to Sarah Mower of *Harper's Bazaar*. "If she doesn't like a sketch, I will cancel it." Mower added, "Even before her hands-on role became so publically apparent, Gianni had always been careful to point out that Donatella was the one who had the idea that the casting of shows should include magazine models. . . . Had it not been for Donatella and her instinct for publicity, the supermodel phenomenon might never have happened."

As time wore on, her design contributions became greater and greater. Then, in 1993, after a runway show in Milan, Donatella joined her brother onstage for the first time. "It was an important public acknowledgment of Ms. Versace's design contribution," according to White, who added that in 1994 "the company began referring to Ms. Versace as co-designer for Gianni Versace." The 1993 show was for Versus and Istante, two lower-priced lines featuring Versace's creations reinterpreted to appeal to younger buyers, and so were perfect for Donatella's design sensibilities.

Soon Donatella had her own studio and was responsible for designing the Versus, Istante, and children's lines as well as accessories, including shoes and handbags. She stayed in charge of the advertising campaigns, and in 1995, she headed up the launch of Versace's new perfume, Blonde. White wrote that this involvement put the company "in an unusual and enviable position. Here are not one but two designers who bear the house's name and vision. There is no other leading design house that can make this claim." Her responsibilities within the company soon grew even greater, however, when Gianni Versace was diagnosed with cancer of the inner ear.

It started when his hearing suddenly grew worse, but when his right cheek began to swell up, Versace knew it was more than just a simple infection. He started chemotherapy in August 1994—and began transferring more creative power to Donatella, just in case. The chemotherapy lasted until October 1995 and was successful; the cancer soon went into remission. In the meantime, however, Donatella had gotten used to being in control. When he came back, according to *Vanity Fair*'s Cathy Horyn, "things broke out into a first-rate clash of egos that Donatella says lasted about six months. 'It was a moment when I didn't feel any communication,' she says, adding that hurt feelings were probably to blame for much of the stalemate. 'Gianni did not feel jealous that I was there,' she says. 'He felt that people were not giving him attention. I love Gianni more than ever.'"

ELEMENTS OF STYLE

I try to test many areas in my work. Maybe in the future I will be completely one look, I don't know that yet, but more and more my fashion is about freedom. But even in freedom, you have control if you have style, if you respect people. I respect the boys with ties, I respect the little boys in Miami with the very loose shirts. Fashion, you know, is dead; style is inside. It's why I wear Versace or why I wear horse meat.

Men who have no legami, no restraints, free. And that's fashion: born every day, change every day. You cannot trust any one design: What's out today is in tomorrow. I remember my mother worked hard to wear all kinds of things to hide the bra and the strap, and now if the bra is not out, it is not fashion. The change is in attitude."

—*Gianni Versace*, Women's Wear Daily

Adding to the tension at the House of Versace was the interrogation of Santo as part of Italy's "Tangentopoli" or "Kickback City" corruption cleanup campaign, which had exposed tax officials who accepted bribes from companies they were auditing. But the greatest source of tension at this time was Donatella's increasing drug use. Elton John was one of the first to confront Versace about it, according to Ball. "Listen, Gianni, people are laughing at Donatella in America," Ball quotes him as saying. "She goes to all of these parties and she's always running out of the room. When she comes back, everyone can see that she's stoned." Versace knew that she had used cocaine, but he did not realize the extent of the problem until she started regularly showing up late to work.

As if to highlight the rift between the siblings, Donatella's designs started growing more distinct from her brother's. In her review of the Versus line in March 1996, Amy Spindler of the *New York Times* wrote: "This season, Ms. Versace went decidedly her own way, borrowing only the vivid sky blue and glowing red from her brother's latest show for a beautiful group of bright leather coats over sheer dresses, epaulet jackets and shoulder dresses. The rest of the collection was recognizable as purely Donatella, with the raucous off-color kaleidoscopic computer prints she has made her signature, a world away from the historic roots of the Florentine-style prints of her brother."

Despite all of the problems, however, Donatella and her brother continued to work closely together, and she would have a big influence on one of the final acts in his career: the move toward more simplicity in his designs.

THE NEW SIMPLICITY

The movement began as early as 1993. "Blurring the lines between couture and ready-to-wear, [Gianni] startled his audience by offering seriously short styles, using graphic stripes in place of his well-known prints and eschewing his usual extravagance in favor of relatively sober clothes," wrote Bernadine Morris in the *New York*

Although she did not have much experience as a designer or seamstress, Donatella's opinions greatly influenced many of Gianni's creative decisions. As his muse, Donatella advised Gianni and pushed him to use well-known models to walk in their runway shows. *Above*, Versace takes the runway with supermodels.

Times. In 1994, he made it his dominant theme for the year. "My overall idea for 1994 is simplicity," he said, as quoted by Minnie Gastel in *The Versace Legend.* He did not see the new movement as a rejection of his past work, but rather as part of his evolution as a designer. "I don't even repudiate my decorative period—the neo-Baroque period," he said. "I've merely moved on."

According to Ball, however, this is one phase of his evolution that did not come naturally to him. "Minimalism was a foreign language to a man who viewed the world in bright, bold colors," she wrote. It was in fact Donatella who recognized the trend and moved the company in that direction. Ball writes: "The models, photographers, and makeup artists she hung out with were crazy about minimalism. Donatella, ever sensitive to new vibes, was soon hooked herself.... She embarked on a campaign to convince her brother to find a way to embrace the minimalist trend."

He did listen to Donatella, and his designs took a turn toward the elegant. The April 17, 1995, cover of *Time* magazine featured Claudia Schiffer in a simple white Versace suit. The *New York Times*'s Spindler wrote: "No designer as established as Mr. Versace in his style and clientele has gone so far so fast in remaking what is his signature. His reason for recreating the house is simple. 'Women,' he said, after the show. 'I live with women, and they say they want something clean and I try.'" Taking as inspiration such elegant icons as Audrey Hepburn and Grace Kelly, Versace managed to create classic-looking designs that were still recognizable as Versace. "Great designers make their names the buzzwords: when it is said that something is 'very Versace,' there is no need to say much else," wrote Spindler after the October 1995 show in Milan. "It was a collection that could be described as 'very Versace,' and one that felt completely in tune with fashion today."

ON TOP OF THE WORLD

Much to Santo's annoyance, the simplicity movement did not extend to his brother's spending habits. In 1995, Gianni Versace spent $7.5 million on a three-story limestone townhouse in Manhattan, then added a two-story addition. He flew master craftsmen out from Milan to work on the renovation, and commissioned art from some of the top artists of the day, including Roy Lichtenstein, Philip Taaffe, and Julian Schnabel.

Santo, the "responsible" one of the three siblings, was in charge of the Versace finances. His brother spent his own money on his

Versace's success brought the family fame and fortune. With his newfound wealth, the designer purchased homes in some of the world's most glamorous cities and began filling these spaces with luxurious, custom-made furniture and decorations. *Above*, the dining room in Versace's Miami home.

lavish lifestyle, but when that ran out, Santo had to use Versace company money to cover him "so that the company—not Gianni personally—became the owner of the houses and art collection," writes Ball. "I never told Gianni what he could really spend," Santo said to Ball. "If I knew he could afford to spend one hundred, I told him he could spend ten. And then he would spend twenty." Gianni Versace, for his part, believed that as the creative force of the Versace brand, he should be able to spend the money however he wanted. "The company is mine!" he said, according to Ball. "I built it and I want to enjoy my money."

The following summer, he convinced Santo to sell him 5 percent of the company, bringing Versace's stake up to 45 percent. In the spring of 1997, Santo sold him another 5 percent, giving Versace a controlling 50 percent share. That same spring, according to Dana Thomas of *Newsweek*, his rift with Donatella came to a head as well. Versace could no longer take their constant battles for power in the design studio. "Enough!" he yelled at her. "I have decided that we will do things differently. I don't want to do this anymore."

In 1996, Versace's cancer was in remission and he had a new lease on life. He was even feeling feisty enough to get off a shot or two in his long-running rivalry with fellow Milanese designer Giorgio Armani. When Armani was quoted as saying that fashion is finished, Versace responded, "At the beginning of each season, there are fashion designers who discover all of a sudden that fashion is dead, perhaps confusing overall appreciation with a personal problem. This time, it is Giorgio Armani's turn, just as he is opening two stores in New York, and not ones which sell records."

In October of that year, he held a party at his New York townhouse to celebrate his twentieth anniversary in the fashion business. Later that month, a new Versace store opened on Fifth Avenue in New York—at 25,000 square feet (2,322.5-square-meters) it was the company's largest store in the world, and the first to house all Versace lines.

At the end of 1996, Versace published *Rock and Royalty*, the latest in his line of fashion and art books that included *Signatures, Do Not Disturb, Vanitas: Designs, Men Without Ties,* and *South Beach Stories.* More good news awaited him with the year-end financials for the Versace group: wholesale sales of all Versace products reached approximately $1 billion worldwide in 1996.

Versace even started getting along better with his family. Gastel quotes Versace as saying, "I feel I've been reborn after my illness. . . . I feel at peace now, very relaxed. I'm fortunate to have a wonderful family. At times we tear each other to pieces, but we always do it in order to create something. We have a pact in which we always reunite, here and now, together. Whatever happens."

He started 1997 with an atelier show that was, as Gastel puts it, "dedicated to lightness and sobriety." "My whole collection should fit in a suitcase," he said. Later in January came the debut of Béjart's ballet *Le presbytère n'a rien perdu de son charme ni le jardin de son éclat* with costumes by Versace. The final collaboration between the two, for the Pitti Immagine Uomo menswear trade fair in Florence in June, was the closest and most imaginative yet. The event, at the Boboli Gardens of the Palazzo Pitti, featured both a performance of the ballet *Barocco Bel Canto* with Versace costumes and a preview of Versace's spring-summer 1998 menswear collection. "I am looking for more creative ways to talk to my customers," Versace told Sara Gay Forden of the *Daily News Record*. To the end, Versace was looking forward and trying to surprise people. The Palazzo Pitti show ended with Naomi Campbell trotting down the runway "with a gun, firing off a few shots—hopefully blanks—into the air," the *Daily News Record* reported. The magazine called it "one of the strongest collections in years."

5

A Tragic Death

After his final couture show in Paris in July 1997, Versace boarded a plane for New York. There he met with bankers at Morgan Stanley to discuss taking his company public. A listing on the stock exchange would give Versace the hundreds of millions of dollars they needed to undertake the ambitious expansion they had planned. According to Dana Thomas of *Newsweek*, at the end of the meeting, Versace jotted this note in the margin of the contract: "It has been fun. It will be even more fun. We'll see you in the fall to set the issue price."

On July 10, he flew from New York back home to Miami. The following Monday night, he went with Antonio and a friend to see the 7:30 P.M. showing of *Contact* starring Jodie Foster, then retired for the evening. The *Miami Herald* reconstructed Versace's next day. When he woke up, he followed his typical morning routine.

ELEMENTS OF STYLE

When, after the analyses, counteranalyses, CAT scans, and so on, I realized that it was possible that at not even fifty years old I could just . . . go, I said to myself, "Well, every day that I live from now on—it's my party," . . . I thought, Benissimo. *If I have to die, I can thank God that I have lived forty-nine fantastic years. I don't have any regrets; I've always done what I wanted. I have a splendid family, a tranquil personal life. I adore the work I do. Besides that, I have the privilege of designing for the theater, and I've gotten to know the greatest artists of this century. I mean everybody, from Rauschenberg to Twombly. I even met Picasso, when I was twenty-two. What more could anyone want?*

—*Gianni Versace, the* New Yorker

He put on his jogging shorts, T-shirt, and flip-flops, then walked to the nearby News Café shortly after 8:00 A.M. Versace was a voracious reader, absorbing as much knowledge and culture as he could. That morning he bought *Entertainment Weekly, Newsweek,* the *New Yorker, People,* and *Vogue* as well as a cup of coffee.

Around 8:40 A.M., he started heading home down Ocean Drive. He and artist Herbert Hofer greeted each other. "He was just walking, enjoying himself," Hofer told the *Herald.*

At 8:44 A.M., Versace reached the steps of Casa Casuarina. As he was unlocking the gate to his palazzo, a young man in shorts and a white cap came up behind him and fired two shots from a .40-caliber handgun to Versace's head. Versace fell to the ground, his face toward the sky.

Antonio, attracted by the sound of the gunshots, ran from the house and was one of the first on the scene. With him was Lazaro Quintana, who had come to play tennis with Antonio. As Antonio reached the sidewalk, he later recounted to Minnie Gastel in *The Versace Legend,* he saw "Gianni lying on the steps in a pool of blood. Then my vision clouds up, a scream bursts from my lips, and I feel like I'm going to keel over." A woman who had witnessed the whole thing pointed out the shooter, and Lazaro gave chase.

At some point, the shooter realized he was being followed, turned and pointed the gun at Lazaro, then continued running. Lazaro spotted a police officer and stopped to tell him what had happened. The officer set off after the gunman.

Soon an ambulance arrived. The medics put Versace inside the ambulance and set to work on him as they drove to Jackson Memorial Hospital. He arrived at the trauma center around 9:15 A.M. The neurosurgeon on duty told the *Herald* that Versace "was in arrest, basically his heart had stopped, and systemically brain dead." Gianni Versace was declared dead at 9:21 A.M. on July 15, 1997.

Antonio meanwhile had to get in a police car to help search for the shooter and so was unable to accompany Versace to the hospital. The gunman had fled down an alley and entered a parking garage. Witnesses say they saw him enter a red Chevrolet truck, change clothes, then leave on foot. The truck belonged to William Reese, a New Jersey cemetery caretaker who had been murdered in May of that year. When police searched the truck, they found bloody clothing underneath it. Inside they found a wallet belonging to Lee Miglin, a Chicago developer who had also been killed in May. The main suspect in both murders as well as two others was 27-year-old Andrew Cunanan. Also in the truck was a passport with Cunanan's name on it. The police now had their suspect for the murder of Gianni Versace.

THE KILLER

A "high-class homosexual prostitute." This is how Cunanan's mother described him in May 1997 when the *Chicago Sun-Times* asked her how Andrew got his money. At that point he was already wanted in connection with the four previous murders—Miglin in

Andrew Cunanan murdered two friends in a jealous rage before embarking on a cross-country murder spree.

Chicago, Reese in New Jersey, and Jeffrey Trail and David Madson in Minnesota.

Cunanan was the youngest of four children. His mother, Mary-Ann, was a stay-at-home mom; his father, Modesto, a Philippines-born stockbroker. Cunanan grew up in a suburb of San Diego and came out as a homosexual when still a teenager. He attended the University of California at San Diego, but dropped out in his freshman year after his father fled to the Philippines to avoid being arrested for embezzling from his stockbrokerage business. Andrew joined his father in the Philippines for a short time before returning to California.

In San Francisco, Cunanan lived off of gifts from the older gay men he dated. "His wealthy lovers gave him the money for his expensive clothes and the $1,000 restaurant tabs he would pick up for groups of friends," according to *Time* magazine's Richard Lacayo. He acquired a reputation for lying—Maureen Orth wrote in *Vanity Fair* that among other things, he claimed that he had dropped out of Yale, that his mother was friends with rock star Deborah Harry, and that he sometimes flew planes for a Filipino senator. He also claimed to have met Gianni Versace at a club in San Francisco in 1990 when Versace was there to design clothes for the San Francisco Opera. Cunanan next moved back to San Diego, where he started using the name Andrew DeSilva, and he began dealing drugs in addition to living off of other wealthy older men.

Things were already going downhill for Cunanan in 1996 when one of those older men he had been living off of, Norman Blachford, broke things off. Earlier that year, Cunanan's boyfriend David Madson, whom he met in San Francisco, had broken up with him. Later, Cunanan's relationship with his best friend, Jeffrey Trail, fell apart as well.

In April 1997, both Madson and Trail were living in Minnesota. Cunanan was drinking heavily by this time and using drugs. On April 25, he flew to Minnesota to visit Madson and Trail. Two days later, Cunanan asked Trail to come over to Madson's apartment. There, for reasons still not entirely clear, Cunanan killed Trail, striking him viciously on the head with a hammer 25 to 30 times. On May 3, two fishermen found Madson's body dumped near a lake about an hour north of Minneapolis. Cunanan had shot him several times in the head and back with a .40-caliber gun.

That same day, Cunanan was in Chicago, where he tortured and killed 72-year-old developer Lee Miglin, stabbing him with gardening shears and slashing his throat. The link, if any, between Cunanan and Miglin is unknown—the Miglin family denied that they knew each other. Madson's red Jeep Cherokee was found nearby a couple of days later.

Miglin's car was found on May 9 next to Finns Point National Cemetery in Pennsville, New Jersey. Nearby was the body of 45-year-old William Reese, the cemetery caretaker. He had been

The Rumor Mill

Immediately after the murder, the media began piecing together Cunanan's time in Miami leading up to the morning of July 15—the hotel he stayed in, the pawn shop where he sold a gold coin belonging to Miglin, the club he went to the night before the killing. What they could not piece together, however, was a motive. From the beginning, rumors abounded. The killing was carried out execution-style, and a dead dove found next to Versace's body was, according to Ball, "taken as a signature of a mafia hit, reviving talk that the Versaces had connections to Calabrian organized crime families." As it turns out, an autopsy of the bird revealed that it was killed by a bullet fragment that had ricocheted off the iron gate.

Another rumor was that Cunanan and Versace had actually known each other, and that Cunanan killed the designer as revenge for giving him AIDS. Orth wrote a book in which she claimed that Versace had AIDS, but Ball writes: "the family released a letter from Gianni's doctor in Milan denying it." Also, according to Ball, "Cunanan's autopsy revealed that he was actually HIV-negative, bursting the theory that he killed Gianni because the designer had infected him." Disproving these and other conspiracy theories, however, got the press no closer to Cunanan's real reason for killing Versace and his other victims.

shot once in the head by the same .40-caliber gun used to kill Madson. Apparently Cunanan killed Reese just to get his red 1995 Chevrolet truck. This is the truck that he would drive to Miami and park in the garage near Versace's South Beach home.

Different people had different theories about why Cunanan went on his murderous spree. An AIDS counselor told the *San Diego Union-Tribune* that Cunanan feared he might have AIDS and said, "If I find out who did this to me, I'm gonna get them." Another theory came from Philip Horne, a close friend of Cunanan's, who told the *Herald*: "[Cunan was] an over-the-hill gay gigolo with a gut, past his prime at 27, recently tossed out of a luxurious home by his wealthy, elderly patron, forced to rent a walk-up efficiency. For someone always driven by a maniacal ego, this was the crushing blow," Horne said.

"The real Cunanan, hidden behind layers of his own lies, has never been easy to find," Lacayo wrote. Nor would anybody get the chance to find the real Cunanan.

AFTER THE MURDER

Almost as soon as the police arrived on the scene of Gianni Versace's murder, the press appeared. Newspaper, television, and magazine reporters from all over the world made their way to Casa Casuarina. Hundreds of curious citizens gathered as well. Police collected as evidence Versace's shoes from the front steps as well as the magazines he had purchased at the News Café and put the items into individual brown paper bags. Firemen then hosed down the steps and sidewalk to wash away the blood. After the police removed the yellow crime scene tape, some from the crowd laid down flowers.

As soon as FBI agents figured out that the red pickup truck in the garage near Versace's mansion belonged to William Reese, they knew the suspect they were looking for in Gianni Versace's murder was Andrew Cunanan. He was already on the FBI's Ten Most Wanted list by that point, with a $10,000 reward offered for

The official Versace memorial mass was held in Milan's famous cathedral, the Duomo. More than 2,000 people attended the service (*above*).

information leading to his capture. It was not until 8:30 that night, however, that the police issued a press release saying that the man they were looking for was Cunanan.

Antonio was still at the police department at this point. After searching the area with police, he answered questions at the crime scene, then he and Lazaro were taken to the station to answer more questions and look through pictures of Cunanan. Though Cunanan had many different looks in the photos, Antonio eventually recognized him in one of them.

Santo and Donatella arrived from Rome the morning after the murder. For days, they and Antonio waited for news of Cunanan's capture. Hundreds of Miami police, Florida state police, and FBI agents worked on the case, and the media closely followed every new development and false lead.

With Cunanan still on the loose, Miami residents remained on edge. Calls poured in to the tip line with false Cunanan sightings. Finally, on July 23, the police got the call they were waiting for. Fernando Carreira, a property caretaker, checked up on a houseboat belonging to one of his clients. The boat was at Indian Creek, about 4 miles (6.4 kilometers) north of Casa Casuarina. Carreira saw that somebody had been living in the boat. As he and his wife searched the boat, they heard a gunshot upstairs. They fled and called the police.

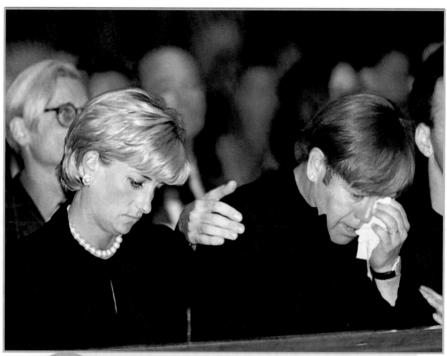

Versace had developed deep friendships with many of his celebrity clients, and his funeral was filled with famous faces. *Above*, Diana, Princess of Wales, and Elton John attend Versace's official memorial mass in Milan.

The police showed up within minutes, with the media close behind. A SWAT team moved in, and though they initially reported not seeing anyone on board, they soon confirmed that they had found a body. Andrew Cunanan had killed himself with a shot to the head from the same .40-caliber gun he had used first on Madson, then on Reese, and then on Versace. One of the largest manhunts in U.S. history had come to a bloody end.

GRIEF AND MOURNING

While the police hunted for Cunanan, friends, family, and fashion world colleagues got on with the business of saying goodbye to Gianni Versace. Words of sympathy and grief poured in from around the world, from celebrity friends such as Sting, Sylvester Stallone, Elton John, and Princess Diana, models such as Kate Moss, designers such as Valentino and Giorgio Armani, as well as fans in the general public. The day after the killing, Versace stores around the globe closed shop in mourning, while an evening mass held in Rome was attended by many from Italy's fashion industry. The city council of Reggio di Calabria declared a day of mourning. On July 18, 700 people packed into Saint Patrick Catholic Church in Miami Beach for a memorial service while many more listened outside.

Antonio, Donatella, and Santo were not at the memorial, however. After holding a private cremation ceremony, they left the night of July 17 for Italy, bringing with them Versace's ashes in a brass urn. They brought the ashes to the cemetery in Moltrasio on Lake Como.

The memorial mass for Gianni Versace was held in the Duomo, Milan's cathedral, on July 22. Shop owners in Milan's golden triangle district closed their stores that day out of respect. More than 2,000 people came to the cathedral, but only 400 close friends received special invitations that let them enter the inner circle of the memorial. "People with 'ordinary' tickets went in through the front door while celebrities, including Carolyn Bessette, wife of John F. Kennedy Jr., were provided with a separate side entrance," explains Lowri Turner in *Gianni Versace: Fashion's Last Emperor*. "Inside the church, the parallel with a fashion show was just as marked. Seating was arranged according to status and personal relationship with the dead designer. The Princess of Wales sat between Elton John and Trudie Styler [Sting's wife] in the family pew with Antonio d'Amico, Santo, Donatella, Paul Beck, and their children, Allegra and Daniel." Across the aisle sat some of the leading designers of the time, including Armani, Gianfranco Ferre, Karl Lagerfeld, and Valentino.

The mass was conducted by Monsignor Luciano Migliavacca. Maurice Béjart gave a reading from the Book of Wisdom, while Sting and Elton John sang the Twenty-third Psalm.

Gianni Versace's ashes were entombed in a mausoleum at the Moltrasio cemetery. The tomb soon became a tourist destination for fashion fans. Turner writes that at one point, an attempt was made to steal the ashes, after which the Versaces installed electronic alarms and hired guards.

Tributes and remembrances followed in the weeks after the funeral. In December, the Metropolitan Museum of Art held an exhibition of Gianni Versace's work at their $2,000-a-plate fund-raising party. Donatella and Santo attended events and accepted condolences while grieving for their brother. They could not let their grief overcome them, however—they had a billion-dollar business to run.

6

The Fall of the
House of Versace

Besides "Who killed Gianni Versace and why?" the other big question immediately after the murder was, "Will the House of Versace survive without Gianni?"

THE AFTERMATH

Many within the fashion industry showed support for Santo and Donatella and expressed their confidence in them. "Gianni was the genius, but they can still go ahead," designer Donatella Girombelli told John Greenwald of *Time*. "It won't be the same [company], but it will still be solid." Bloomingdale's fashion director Kal Ruttenstein told Greenwald, "Versace's team knows how to do the look."

Santo already was in charge of the financial side of the company, and his brother's battle with cancer resulted in his handing off more of the design duties to Donatella. Taking the company public would have to wait—investors would likely be too nervous to put money into a company that had just lost its leader—but perhaps not for long. Jennifer Steinhauer of the *New York Times* wrote that "the company may well be strong enough that after a period to regroup it will be in position to begin its long-anticipated initial public offering as early as next year."

Donatella and Santo did their part to reassure the public as well, releasing a statement two days after the murder that read: "[T]he indomitable spirit, the amazing vitality and the faith in creativity that makes Gianni Versace so important to everyone is something that we are completely committed to and most capable of continuing."

On the personal front, more bad news arrived just weeks later. On August 31, 1997, Donatella heard that Princess Diana had died early that morning in a car crash in Paris. Then, in September, another shock awaited with the reading of Versace's will. Much to everyone's surprise, Versace left his entire 50 percent share of the company to his 11-year-old niece, Allegra. To her brother, Daniel, he left his art collection (though later a judge ruled that the collection actually belonged to the company, not Versace himself, and so could not be willed to Daniel). Antonio received a monthly payment of about $29,000 and the right to live in Versace's properties in Milan, Miami, and New York. Versace left nothing for Donatella, Santo, or Santo's children. Ball writes that at the end of the reading, Santo told Antonio, "I think you had better find yourself a lawyer."

After that, "Donatella completely erased me from the picture," Antonio told Ball. Santo and Donatella later reached an agreement with Antonio to give him a one-time payment plus a company-owned apartment in Milan. A couple of weeks later, "Antonio was escorted out of the atelier by a Versace security guard, without a word from Santo or Donatella," says Ball.

Despite all the tension and drama, Donatella managed to finish the designs that her brother had started for the spring-summer collection in time for the runway show on October 9. She brought

After Gianni's death, Donatella and Santo wasted no time in getting back to business. It was up to Donatella to take on Gianni's design responsibilities and pull together the collection he had been working on when he died. With the help of several young designers, Donatella put on a show that honored Gianni (*above*).

in help in the form of young designers, many from London's Central Saint Martins College of Art and Design. Together they worked tirelessly to pull the collection together.

Celebrity friends such as Demi Moore, Cher, Boy George, Rupert Everett, and Donna Karan came to the show to support Donatella. The night opened with laser lights spelling out a message: "This show is dedicated to our brother Gianni's love of work and to our entire staff, whose incredible love and devotion was so precious to our brother and means so much to us. We thank each and every one of them." After the show, Donatella stood onstage and accepted the crowd's enthusiastic cheers with tears on her face. Amy M. Spindler of the *New York Times* reports that Donatella told Giorgio Armani backstage, "I can barely stand, I'm shaking so badly."

Reviews were positive if not glowing. Spindler wrote that the show for Versus "was exactly as it should be: it was fine. If it were too sound, the judgmental fashion insiders might doubt the sincerity of her mourning. If it were unsound, they might doubt her ability to make the house strong enough to go on." *WWD* wrote: "Was it a perfect collection? No. There were a few awkward fits.... Yet this was no neophyte effort, but a bold, smart and well-polished presentation."

The stress of her first solo collection was behind her, but the grief of losing her brother and the responsibility of carrying the company forward weighed heavily on Donatella.

THE DECLINE OF DONATELLA

Donatella first tried cocaine when she was 32 years old. Then, as she told Sally Singer of *Vogue*, "I just kept doing it, every time I was in New York, in Los Angeles, mostly at parties. I didn't feel I was addicted. I was just having fun." Gianni Versace did not do drugs, but he never directly confronted his sister about her cocaine habit. When her problem got worse, however, and Donatella started showing up late to work, he could no longer completely ignore the problem. "It doesn't matter what you do, but you have to know how to do it and when to do it," he told her.

When her brother died, Donatella gave up drugs for a few months. "I stopped using cocaine because of what happened," she told Singer. "I couldn't go late to work, because Gianni wasn't there. I had to organize my company, my family.... But it wasn't as though I was going to stop my behavior forever. I wish I had."

When she started using cocaine again, she mixed in other drugs as well—Halcion, Valium, Ativan, and Rohypnol. She no longer did drugs openly at parties and fashion shows, but instead, "I started doing it alone, which was even more sad," she said.

Through this period, she still managed to lead the design for the company. She canceled Versace's haute-couture show in Paris in January 1998—the first one the company missed since Versace's debut there in 1990—but in the year following his death, she designed a total of six collections for the Gianni Versace and Versus labels. She received some good reviews, "although she suspects at least some of that has been out of compassion," according to Daniel Peres of *WWD*.

The reviews for her first couture show in July 1998 were not as compassionate, however. *WWD* said the clothes were "a somewhat peculiar lot, combining moments of high chic with others that looked as if a few bats had been let loose in the belfry."

Things might have been seeming to turn around with her runway shows in October 1998—*WWD* said the collection "looked great" while Anne-Marie Schiro of the *New York Times* called it "the best collection she's done on her own since the death of her brother Gianni"—but it was not enough to convince the public. Profits plummeted to $8.8 million in 1998, a huge drop compared to 1997's $46.2 million, even discounting the $23.4 million from Gianni Versace's life insurance policy. The company placed some of the blame on the Asian financial crisis, but things grew even worse in 1999.

As the collections started to look less and less like what people had come to expect from Versace, retailers worried about shoppers buying the clothes. In March 1999, Dana Thomas of *Newsweek International* wrote that up to that point, "Donatella has virtually erased the look that he spent a lifetime creating. Gone are the sexy-hooker dresses, the fun and flashy designs that made Gianni so famous. In their place: softer, sleeker corporate suits and gauzy gowns. Where Gianni favored bold primary colors topped off with gaudy beads or rhinestones, Donatella prefers floral prints and feminine hues." Suzanne Patneaude, vice president for women's designer apparel at Nordstrom, told Thomas, "We love what Donatella does on the runway—it's so young and vibrant and fresh—but the customer who can afford Versace isn't 25."

Donatella's personal life suffered as well. She and Paul officially separated in June 1999. According to Ball, she got into a big fight with Santo at a charity runway show that same month, during which Santo screamed at her, "Those clothes are disgusting! I can't even look at them!" Her personal spending and her spending for the company got out of control as well, despite the company's declining sales. When asked about her breakup with Paul, she told Ariel Levy of *New York* magazine, "I have been living with a lot of pain in my life: private problems, family problems. I found an easy way to numb everything . . . drugs."

To make matters worse, the stress took its toll on Allegra as well, beginning just weeks after her uncle's murder. Ball writes that "just as Donatella was preparing her debut runway show, Allegra simply stopped eating. As the fall wore on, the girl grew alarmingly thin." She was suffering from anorexia, and her health was deteriorating.

Meanwhile, sales at the company continued to fall, down 7 percent to $399 million in 1999. Santo started a restructuring program to turn the company around, including signing new deals such as opening the first Palazzo Versace resort in Australia, boosting its perfume division and accessories and home

ELEMENTS OF STYLE

Always the difference between me and Gianni was that I was much more for risking than he was. He was established—he didn't need to risk anymore in a way. I have played a lot and experimented. But I don't regret any of it. Everything I did helped the current collection to be what it is now. I got bad reviews. And I was ready for it. I knew I was going to be criticized. But I always felt that I couldn't simply repeat [what Gianni did]. In the three years since Gianni died, fashion has changed so much. Big companies have merged, the supermodel thing is over. I had to find a new way to keep up with the times.

Women want to make a statement, but they're much more refined about it now. They don't need to cover themselves in a business suit to work. They're in much more powerful positions in business, and they don't need to fake it, you know—to be bare-faced in flat shoes, to dress like a man in a man's world. It's not a man's world anymore.

—*Donatella Versace*, Harper's Magazine

collections, and selling off his brother's Miami mansion and its contents for $19 million.

The plan seemed to work at first, and this combined with some more good reviews led to a recovery in 2000. "The most remarkable aspect of the Versace revival," wrote Zoe Heller in *Harper's Bazaar*, "is Donatella's genesis as chief designer of the house. After three years of very public trial and error, during which she sought, somewhat desperately, to establish a direction for Versace in the post-Gianni era, her last two collections have seen her flowering."

The recovery was short-lived, however. The terrorist attacks of September 11, 2001, left all of the fashion industry struggling to find the right response. Speaking to *WWD* about her October 2001 collection, Donatella said, "I thought maybe I should make a more sober collection, with no color. But then I thought, to give in to that, the terrorists have won, if we stop doing what we do. Women want to be beautiful."

The confidence she displayed when talking to the press, however, hid her personal turmoil. "Donatella began sleeping until lunchtime and often didn't turn up at Via Gesú until mid-afternoon," Ball writes. "She withdrew more and more, leaving her personal assistants to run interference with staff members, journalists, and friends." Both Donatella and her company were sliding toward ruin.

HITTING BOTTOM

In 2002, Maya Rudolph started doing an impersonation of Dona-tella on *Saturday Night Live*. In the skit, Rudolph poked fun at Donatella's extravagance ("Let's go to my private jet and go to that fancy McDonald's in Monte Carlo.") Donatella claimed to love the impersonation, but she could not have been as good-natured about the ribbing she received in January 2003 when she landed on fash-ion critic Richard Blackwell's list of the worst-dressed celebrities: "Resembles a flash-fried Venus stuck in a Miami strip mall."

It was a sign of the times for Donatella, whose drug addiction and personal spending reached new heights while the company's finances spiraled downward. The year 2002 saw a net loss of $6.8 mil-lion for Versace as it cut advertising, merged some collections, and shut stores. In January 2003, Versace ended its haute-couture runway show, which Orla Healy of the *Independent* (Ireland) wrote "added to the swirling impression that Casa Versace is losing its edge."

That year, accountants responsible for watching the com-pany's finances demanded that "Donatella reimburse Versace for her personal expenditures and [warned] that the house's soaring costs threatened to destroy the company," according to Ball, but "Donatella still refused to reimburse the house for the expendi-tures." *WWD* described Versace as the "famous but financially struggling house."

Donatella's life began to fall apart as she struggled to establish her own creative vision with her designs. Her marriage failed, her daughter developed an eating disorder, and Donatella's drug use increased during this period.

Sales in 2003 dropped another 17.2 percent to $486.4 million. The company entered a deal to restructure its debts, laid off about 200 people, and closed more stores in 2004. Donatella in the meantime was planning out her cocaine binges, according to *Vogue*'s Singer, "doing meetings in advance with her team, clearing her desk, asking that work be sent to the house when she wasn't 'feeling well' for two or three days."

"Cocaine is such a bad drug," Donatella said to Singer. "It lies to you every time. You think you can control it. If I was doing less—two lines, three lines, because that's nothing for me—I thought I'd stopped. For me that was stopping."

Her relationships with her friends suffered as she withdrew into herself. She began avoiding her true friends such as Elton

Armani on Top

While Gianni Versace was alive, his greatest rival in the fashion world was Giorigo Armani. Their design styles were almost polar opposites of each other's—Versace's flashy and Armani's conservative—and their runway shows matched. The press loved playing up the rivalry, especially when one made sharp comments about the other. "I prefer a woman who's dressed badly but who is free, to an idiot wearing Giorgio Armani," Minnie Gastel quotes Gianni Versace as saying. "They were the salt and pepper you needed to give some zip to fashion," former *Donna* editor in chief Gisella Borioli told Gastel.

In the wake of Gianni Versace's murder, however, the rivalry largely disappeared as the Versace brand struggled while Giorgio Armani experienced the kind of success that Gianni Versace once aspired to. In 2000, Armani celebrated the twenty-fifth anniversary of his company. The Guggenheim Museum in New York held an Armani exhibit complete with a star-studded opening party. Armani's fortunes were rising as well, with retail sales in excess of $3 billion in 1999. In 2000, he launched a new joint venture with the Zegna Group, a cosmetics line, and a home fashion store, and opened a new megastore in Milan. Meanwhile, as the 1990s drew to a close, Versace's sales were shrinking. According to Ball, "For Santo, the incessant coverage of Armani's year-long anniversary bash and the stratospheric valuations bandied about for his old rival were painful reminders of what Versace could have become."

John, Elizabeth Hurley, and Madonna. "You think you don't need anybody else," she told Singer. "You think you're the beginning and end of the world. That's the worst thing."

In March 2004, she started using cocaine on a daily basis, Singer wrote. "When you use cocaine every day, your brain doesn't work anymore," Donatella said. She experienced dramatic mood swings, she terrified Allegra and Daniel with her erratic behavior, and she even started hearing voices.

Realizing that she had hit bottom, she finally sent out a cry for help.

INTO REHAB

On June 9, 2004, Elton John played a concert at the Stadio Granillo in di Calabria. Donatella watched her friend's show from the side of the stage—crying and shaking the whole time. "It was a sign," Elton John told Singer. "She was showing me herself as a mess, in her hometown, at her worst. It was a brave thing for her to do."

The next day, Elton John arranged an intervention. As it turned out, the only day he had available on his calendar was June 30, Allegra's birthday. Elton was not initially invited to the party, a private dinner for friends and family at the palazzo on Via Gesù in Milan, but he arranged to be there with Paul, Allegra, Santo, and some close friends. When Elton walked in, according to Ball, Donatella knew that something was up. Ball writes that Elton told Donatella, "[W]e're not forcing you, but you need to go to rehab. There's a plane waiting for you." Those at the intervention communicated to Donatella the harm her addiction was doing to those around her as well as to the company. Talking late into the night, they were able to get through to her. "She changed out of her evening gown, took off her jewelry, and put on a jogging suit," writes Ball. "Then she headed to the airport, where she boarded a private plane headed for Arizona. For much of the long trip, she sobbed." Donatella told Singer, "I remember during the trip thinking I didn't get enough information about where I was going. I am such a control freak."

Her destination in Arizona was the Meadows rehab clinic in the town of Wickenburg. It was known for treating many celebrities who liked its remote location and staff trained to keep out paparazzi. Donatella received tough love at the clinic, with a set of strict rules about how to dress, when to get up, and when to go therapy. She was diagnosed with severe depression, and a nurse came to check on her daily.

The company confirmed the fact that Donatella had entered rehab but did not say where. Toward the end of her stay, Allegra and Daniel traveled to Arizona to visit her at the clinic. "I think I never cried so much as when the children left," she confessed to Ariel Levy. "So for me to be so open now, so close together, I feel so much joy."

She stayed at the clinic for five weeks and emerged sober. "All she talks about, and all I talked about when I got sober, was how great it is to be sober," Elton John said to Singer. "I'm keeping an eye on her. I think she's really got it.... I'm so happy to have her back in my life." As Donatella put it, "I'm very determined that I don't want to feel that way again."

7

Back from the Brink

The party at which Donatella's intervention occurred was in celebration of Allegra's eighteenth birthday—the day on which she officially became an adult and took control of her 50 percent share in Versace. In 1997, the year her uncle died, Versace sales totaled about $1 billion. In 2003, they were less than half that. The company Allegra inherited was vastly different from the one her uncle left her. Plagued by unreliable clothing deliveries and being dropped by stores such as Bergdorf Goodman, Versace fell from No. 2 among Italian fashion companies in 1997 to No. 10 in 2004.

ALLEGRA TURNS 18
Despite the big new responsibility landing in her lap, Allegra did what she could to enjoy her eighteenth birthday. In addition to the

Gianni's will was a surprise to both his family and friends, as he bequeathed his share of the Versace company to his niece, Allegra (*above*). Donatella's daughter was to inherit Gianni's shares when she turned 18. Allegra took her role seriously, and, when she came of age, she began attending business meetings and learning all she could about the company.

small private party on her actual birthday, she held a larger bash on June 14 at the Alcatraz nightclub in Milan, complete with customized T-shirts for her friends, a big buffet, and a performance by hip-hop star Pharrell Williams.

As her big birthday came and went, she kept her intentions regarding her involvement in the company a secret to some extent. It was known that she planned on attending Brown University in the United States in the fall, which would mean a lower level of involvement in Versace, but she would still have the deciding vote at company board meetings.

At the next shareholder meeting, held in July 2004, Donatella and Santo voted to sign off on the company's year-end results for 2003. Allegra attended the meeting but abstained from the vote. According to the *Daily News Record*: "[H]er attendance at the meeting indicates she is taking seriously her new responsibilities as Versace's largest single shareholder." Versace interim chief executive officer Daniele Ballestrazzi told the *Daily News Record*, "She needs time to understand the figures." In October of that year, a proud Donatella told *WWD*, "[S]he's a very smart girl—and I'm not saying that because I'm her mother. Everyone says it. She wants to know everything about the business, and we talk about business as mother and daughter."

As she educated herself about the business, Allegra also focused on her studies at Brown. She also held ambitions to become an actress. Allegra was never expected to come in and save the company, of course. With sales sinking and with Donatella recently out of rehab and sober, there was finally both recognition and acceptance of the need to bring in some new leadership.

THE NEW CEO

Allegra chose not to sit in on the Versace board members' meeting held on August 26, 2004. At that meeting, Santo was reconfirmed as president of the company, with Donatella set to be reconfirmed as vice president at another meeting on September 2. The big announcement at the meeting, however, was that Giancarlo Di Risio would become the company's new chief executive officer (CEO).

In one of his former business lives, Di Risio was a tractor sales-man, but more recently he was CEO of the luxury goods compa-nies IT Holding and Fendi. He was known more for his business know-how than for his creative spark. In one of his first moves at Versace, Di Risio, according to Deborah Ball, "gave Donatella and her team clear directives for the October 2004 show. He wanted a cleaner, more sophisticated collection. . . . They had to pay closer attention to the fit of the clothes and include more wearable, basic items—not just eveningwear made for willowy models—and fol-low a strict design calendar so that the factory had time to make the clothes." Donatella told *WWD* that she had most of the design for the October show done before she entered rehab, but she did confirm that she would no longer show haute couture on the run-way, opting instead to integrate a few couture pieces into each col-lection. "I love couture," she said, "but I am also a very modern person. The idea of an entire collection of dresses that can take up to three months to make does not fit into the reality of the business right now." And though Di Risio "called an end to lavishing clothes on celebrities willy-nilly," as Ball puts it, he still saw the market-ing value of designing specialty creations for the Oscars and other celebrity red-carpet appearances.

Whether or not Donatella's spring collection for the October show was a direct result of Di Risio's vision of a cleaner, leaner Ver-sace, the designer and the CEO appeared to be on the same page. "It was a more mature collection, it was for the market, for the real world," Donatella said to *WWD*. "And I took a softer approach. The fabrics were softer, lighter, more liquid."

The new direction paid off. *WWD* called the collection "delib-erately low-key . . . some of the simplest clothes ever to hit her runway" and delivered the verdict, "[f]or the most part, it worked beautifully." Cathy Horyn of the *New York Times*, noting Dona-tella's apparent new optimism after emerging from rehab, wrote:

Versace on the Red Carpet

Gianni Versace was known for creating stunning gowns for celebrities to wear to the Oscars, the Grammys, and other red-carpet events. That did not change with Donatella at the design helm. If anything, designing for the red carpet has taken on new significance during Donatella's reign as the company works to maintain its high-end image.

When the department store Debenhams conducted its poll to determine the "Top 20 Most Iconic Red Carpet Dresses," the Elizabeth Hurley safety pin dress unsurprisingly topped the list. Versace had five of those top 20 dresses, more than any other design house. Of those, three were designed by Donatella: Catherine Zeta Jones's 1999 Oscars dress (No. 4), Jennifer Lopez's 2000 Grammys dress (No. 5), and Penelope Cruz's 2007 Oscars dress (No. 15). When *Entertainment Weekly* compiled "The Best Style: 1990–2010" list, the Cruz gown came out on top. "With one swoop of her Atelier Versace gown, Cruz set the standard for Oscar fashion," the magazine reported.

These showstoppers continued to prove their value as powerful marketing tools as well. Stephanie Miller of *Second City Style* called Jennifer Lopez's deep-V green dress "the most photographed dress, ever." Donatella told *WWD* that when Lopez wore the dress, "she was mentioned 82 times the next day between the news and the newspapers. Even if we didn't sell that special dress, that print was done in T-shirts, bags, shoes. The next two days, we were sold out of everything."

"[T]o look at her clothes was to perceive a quality of grown-up experience, an intuitive understanding about women, missing from other designers' collections."

Besides the new design aesthetic, things were different for Donatella both in the atelier and at home. No more showing up to work at noon or later—"I still don't get to the office at 8 A.M.," she said in an interview with *WWD*. "I go in 10, 10:30—quarter to 11 is even better. I'm not a saint—yet." And she worked hard at mending her fractured relationships with Allegra and Daniel. Ball writes: "Donatella pushed for business meetings to end on time so that she could curl up on the sofa at home to watch a soccer game with [Daniel] or listen to him play in his high school band Nucleus." "I spend a lot of time with him, and he is my greatest critic on the collections," Donatella told *WWD*. "I'm actually petrified of what he's going to say about them."

To help out with company financials, Donatella and Santo put the Versace town house in New York up for sale in October 2004, followed by an auction of the last of Gianni Versace's art collection, and then the sale of the remainder of the original Versace headquarters on Via della Spiga in Milan. The company continued launching new products as well, such as the Versace Collezioni men's line and the Crystal Noir fragrance, which rang up about $36,000 in sales for Harrods in London the day it launched, thanks to an in-store autograph-signing session by Donatella.

Other components of Di Risio's plans to turn the company around included more licensing deals (such as for its beauty and watch businesses) and addressing the problem of slow deliveries to stores. "Di Risio didn't do anything brilliant," a former Versace executive told *Newsweek*. "He did all the things that had been talked about for years, but suddenly Donatella was sober and stopped fighting it."

"Versace chief executive officer Giancarlo Di Risio said that 2004 marked a turning point for the company," *WWD* reported. That turnaround continued through 2005. The company started the year with an ad campaign featuring Madonna. A few months later came another auction, this time for 221 antiques from the Via Gesú palazzo. Meanwhile, writes Ball, Donatella's "collections grew stronger each season, finding a balance between Versace's signature sexiness and polished, pulled-together sophistication. She focused more on monochrome tailored clothing."

A new CEO of Versace was brought in to help turn the company around and increase sales. Donatella was given firm orders to focus less on outrageous, stunning designs that were difficult to wear. She refocused and concentrated on the fit and the materials used to make the clothing. Sales improved as she successfully adapted the Versace look to the current trends in the fashion industry.

To signal a new start for Versace, Di Risio approved a redesign of all Versace shops. The new layout had a cleaner look and made more space for eyeglasses, bags, and other accessories.

The groundwork for the company's comeback was laid. Now it was just a matter of seeing if Versace's customers would return.

SIGNS OF RECOVERY

The Versace revival was helped along by consistently good reviews for Donatella's collections in 2005. She even branched out further into Gianni Versace territory during this time by designing costumes, in this case for a short-film remake of Gore Vidal's *Caligula* by Italian artist Francesco Vezzoli.

The company reported better-than-expected results for 2005, and started off 2006 strong by completing a six-month renovation of its 20,000-square-foot (1,858-square-meter) flagship store on Fifth Avenue in Manhattan.

More importantly, Donatella's designs seemed to keep clicking with the public and with reviewers. Cathy Horyn of the *New York Times*, reviewing Donatella's runway show in February 2006, wrote: "The shapes completely conform to the fast, unencumbered lifestyle of a lot of young women, and that Ms. Versace didn't throw on extra luxury details but instead concentrated on proportion and fit was a smart way to move the brand forward." Guy Trebay of the *New York Times* called it "a show some said had put her struggling house back on the fashion map." In November 2006, she kept the ball rolling. Bridget Foley of *WWD* wrote at the time that "she has emerged as one of the strongest creative forces in fashion, with her spring 2007 collection being widely hailed as among the best in Milan."

Now that Versace "had reclaimed its design DNA," as Trebay put it, the design house made a decision to focus on luxury. In January 2007, Donatella introduced Gianni Versace Couture, a line of handmade suits, dress shirts, leather accessories, and more to be sold in select Versace stores around the world. The luxury line was to feature limited-edition pieces, some limited to just one model, and offer customers the chance to order made-to-measure creations.

The next month, Donatella scored another publicity win when she and Gianni were picked to be the ninth and tenth recipients of the Rodeo Drive Walk of Style Award. Started in 2003, the awards recognize people who have made marks in the worlds of fashion

Versace has always been a symbol of a professional type who can risk changing through the times, and Gianni was famous for taking risks and breaking rules. But since Gianni died in 1997, fashion has changed tremendously. For me, it was a dilemma: how to maintain the Versace DNA but at the same time keep updating the Versace style. Versace had been known as the most glamorous and most feminine fashion house, but we moved into a minimalist period, and I was looking for how do I keep Versace up to date. I got to my role right after a tragic event, the death of my brother, so . . . I was very insecure for a while because my brother was a genius, and I was not ready for the role when that happened. I took a certain time to find my way.

My life has changed a lot recently. . . . What I kept with me from the fast life is how fortunate I am to see so many beautiful and glamorous people attending those fantastic parties, and to give my attention to a person entering the room, how they make an entrance, how they make a statement. I now lead a much quieter life, and you see it in my daywear clothes, which are the consequence. But I still enjoy a party.

—*Donatella Versace*, WWD

and entertainment. Similar to the Hollywood Walk of Fame, plaques with the siblings' names were placed in the sidewalk of Rodeo Drive in Hollywood.

Despite this, all was not well in the House of Versace. In March 2007, Donatella and Paul issued a statement confirming that Allegra had anorexia. The statement came in response to media coverage saying that Allegra had been hospitalized for the disease. In their statement, Donatella and Paul said that they "wish to make it clear that their daughter, Allegra, is not at the present time a patient in a hospital of any type, but is residing at her private address and her state of health is stable. . . . Allegra has been battling anorexia, a very serious disease, for many years. She is

The Versace aesthetic was based on the concept of luxury, but as the world entered a recession in late 2008, luxury goods were no longer selling. The company had to refocus its efforts just to stay in business.

receiving the best medical care possible to help overcome this illness and is responding well."

Then in July came the tenth anniversary of Gianni Versace's death. Milan marked the occasion with a commemorative ballet by Maurice Béjart, a fashion scholarship in Gianni Versace's name, and billboards throughout the city displaying sketches of his theatrical costumes. Early the next year, Donatella and Santo decided to sell Villa Fontanelle in Milan. They sold it to a Russian millionaire for $46 million and moved Gianni Versace's ashes to Via Gesú.

The downside of the recovery was the toll Di Risio's measures took on the size of the company. While it was no longer losing money, Versace reported sales in 2006 that were just one-fifth the size of Giorgio Armani's. Ball writes: "Versace was off life support, but it was still a shadow of its former self." In 2007, sales were about $400 million—less than half of what they were the year Gianni Versace died.

In the face of the smaller sales numbers, the company continued its focus on luxury. March 2008 saw the delivery of the first Versace-designed customized helicopters for Italy's AgustaWestland. Versace had signed deals to custom design interiors for Techniques d'Avant Gard's private planes and with Lamborghini for cars, and in May 2008, agreed to design the interior of a residential high-rise in Panama City. An even more exclusive deal came later that year when Versace was picked to design the condominium interiors, common areas, and a luxury spa at the 41-story Clock Tower at Five Madison Avenue in New York, with Donatella personally designing the building's two-story restaurant.

THE RECESSION STRIKES

As Donatella was signing all these high-end deals to establish Versace as a luxury brand, the world was sinking into a colossal financial crisis. The worry became how many people would be left who could afford luxury items, including expensive clothes. The problem was not unique to Versace; it affected the whole fashion industry. Some critics saw luxury-goods providers as being out of touch. In September 2008, the *New York Times*'s Horyn asked the question, "What makes people think that a $3,000 dress with a rash of zippers at the neck can take peoples' minds off an economic crisis or their children's shrinking college funds? Even if Ms. Versace's collection on Thursday night was good—just to deal with the concerns of the totally clueless—it wasn't that good. . . . [S]ome of us left the Versace show—and the Italian spring collections, which ended that evening—with the sense that everything had suddenly come off the rails."

Seemingly unfazed by such criticism or the global financial crisis itself, Donatella launched a new luxury perfume in October 2008. Called Gianni Versace Couture, the fragrance cost $2,100 for a 3.4-fluid-ounce (100-milliliter) bottle. Reality started to sink in soon afterward, however. While the company's sales rose slightly in 2008, its profits shrank by more than 30 percent. Di Risio said that that was more or less in line with what they were expecting, but according to Luisa Zargani of *WWD*, "Di Risio said Versace had begun to feel the effects of the downturn 'a little' in the last three months of 2008."

In 2009, Versace started reaching out to new customers. In February, the company launched Home e-boutique, its first online store. Later that month, it relaunched the Versus line. Donatella and Santo also decided to sell off more of their brother's estate, auctioning off art, sculptures, and furniture from the house on Lake Como.

These measures were not enough, however, and in May, the siblings hired consultancy firm Bain and Company to come up with a three-year plan. This started rumors that Donatella and Di Risio were no longer seeing eye to eye on the direction of Versace. The company issued a statement denying the "professional relationship between the company and its CEO has been terminated," but a month later, Di Risio announced that he was resigning.

Just a week later, Versace hired Di Risio's replacement, Gian Giacomo Ferraris. In his first three months on the job, Ferraris put in place a restructuring plan, closed stores in Japan, and cut 350 jobs, or about 25 percent of the workforce, with a goal of making the company profitable again in 2011. He also "stressed quality and service will remain untouched because he sees Versace as a fashion luxury brand, with apparel accounting for the bulk of sales," wrote Ilari Alessandra of *WWD*.

On the design side, Donatella worked to keep the Versace look modern. "Fashion is struggling to define itself today," she told rock musician Lenny Kravitz, who interviewed her for *Interview* magazine. "For me, I'm concentrating more on fabrics, on the technological aspect of fabrics. . . . What I personally think has come to define these years up until 2009 is fabrics. Technology and fabrics. It's just not quite strong enough yet to see it."

For new design ideas, she turned to music—her "main influence," as she told Kravitz—as well as movies. In September 2009, Donatella took inspiration from Tim Burton's film *Alice in Wonderland* for a collection that won praise from critics. *WWD* wrote:

"A little 'Alice in Wonderland' and a whole lot of classic Versace. The combination made for a terrific spring romp from Donatella Versace." Suzy Menkes of the *New York Times* called it "the first show she has done that captured absolutely the witty and lively spirit of her late brother, Gianni, but with the sexy clothes given a bold, feminist perspective."

At the same time, she looked to the past with the help of young Scottish designer Christopher Kane, with whom she collaborated on Versus. "Under the creative eye of Donatella Versace, Christopher Kane dipped into the Versus archives," *WWD* wrote. The resulting collection featured such classic Versace elements as safety pins and chain mail. Menkes wrote: "The Versus collaboration seemed a perfect fit—literally in the cute, full-skirted dresses and figuratively in the match with Gianni Versace's heritage . . . a sleek and chic amalgam of Versus vintage and new."

In February 2010, Donatella looked to the movies again for inspiration, this time to *Tron Legacy*, set to release later that year. Again, it was a mix of looking backward and forward for Donatella, and again, it seemed to click. "It was as though Donatella Versace had been waiting for this moment to project her late brother Gianni's heritage from the hard-edged, metal mesh of the 1980s into the 21st-century digital age," according to Menkes. "It made for a cracking good show, as sharp as the laser beams that raked the room and as high gloss as the models' slicked hair."

More raves followed for the Versus collection that month as well. The lesson from Donatella's "lost years" of cocaine addiction, however, is that positive reviews are no guarantee of strong sales. With economies around the globe slow to recover, the financial situation of fashion houses such as Versace—particularly those trying to maintain an image of luxury—remains in question. If Donatella's life has taught her anything, though, it is adaptability. "For me, life is about chapters," she told Guy Trebay of the *New York Times*. "Die and born again, die and born again. It's the story of my life."

8

The Versace Legacy

No matter how many chapters or lives Donatella has left in the fashion business, the House of Versace has left its stamp on the industry and culture at large. According to Gianni Versace, one of his earliest contributions came at his first American show, at Studio 54 in 1977: "I think," he told *People* magazine, "that I was the first to bring back padded shoulders, because six months after my collection the fashion journalists came back from Paris saying everybody had copied them."

THE CULTURAL IMPACT

After Gianni Versace's death, and again upon the tenth anniversary of his death, fashion historians and critics assessed his contributions and his place in history. "His talent, a gift for innovative cut, was eclipsed by his celebrity: by the time of his death, he was more

While many remember Gianni Versace as just a designer, there are those who believe he was the first one to fully fuse the world of fashion and celebrity. His ability to turn something vulgar into something glamorous and beautiful thrilled fashion's elite and turned heads in Hollywood.

famous for the company he kept than for the clothes he designed," wrote Holly Brubach in the August 10, 1997, issue of the *New York Times*. "And yet," she continued, "when historians look back on our era, Versace will indeed stand as a pivotal figure for a number of other reasons—chief among them that he legitimized vulgarity. . . . In fashion, thanks to Versace, the issue of whether something is in good taste or in bad taste is now moot."

Closely tied to the charges of vulgarity were Versace's links to the worlds of rock and roll and celebrity in general. Gianni and Donatella Versace were the first designers to turn their runway shows into loud rock-and-roll spectacles, the first to fill their front rows with rock stars such as Bruce Springsteen, Sting, and Elton John, and with movie stars such as Sylvester Stallone and Demi Moore. What became known as classic Versace elements—loud prints, leather, metal, and safety pins—helped reinforce the links to rock and roll in particular.

"Versace fused the cults of celebrity and style," wrote *Time* magazine. "He hastened the transformation of fashion from a rarefied interest of the elite into an object of bottomless mass-cultural fascination. Remember, there weren't always MTV style awards or accountants who can identify the faces in *Harper's Bazaar* or makeup artists with best-selling coffee-table books." Gianni and Donatella Versace's invention of the super-model played into this as well. "By using Supermodels, Versace helped newspapers and TV accept fashion," stylist David Hayes explained to Lowri Turner.

While Donatella was known for building up the celebrity relationships, Gianni was always quick to point out that he was strongly influenced by and likewise influenced the world of theater. Stephanie Miller of *Second City Style* explains, "He confirmed his belief in visual entertainment through his collaborations with theater and ballet producers Richard Strauss and Maurice Béjart." His projects with Béjart in particular resulted in some of Versace's favorite creations, and they were

ELEMENTS OF STYLE

People who think fashion is merely superficial are so blind. It is an integral part of culture. Besides, dressing well shows a certain cultivation and intelligence in understanding the balances of color and form. It is food for fantasy. If I had a baby, I'd want her or him to learn about the quality of silk, of cashmere. Why is it acceptable for cultured people to learn the quality of wine, or antiques, but not to understand fabric? Life is a mixture of quality and knowledge. Why should that not include fashion?

Fashion can never go too far, because its purpose is to make people happy, not to be right or wrong. Only stupid people cling to tradition. I think long skirts are for young people, but all this fuss playing with lengths is just to show women that anything is possible as long as it makes you feel good about yourself. Freedom is what fashion should be about. Long pants, short skirt—whatever you want, as long as it has quality and taste. It is so important to be original.

—*Gianni Versace,* Interview *magazine*

the centerpieces of exhibitions and tributes while he was alive and long after his death.

Pieces such as these highlighted the creativity that helped make Gianni Versace famous. This creativity carried over to his lines for the public as well, and it had a major influence on fashion. "Try to imagine your wardrobe without the jolt of a print, the vitality of a stiletto, the glamorous bric-a-brac of chains and doodads," wrote Cathy Horyn of the *New York Times*. "This was Versace's doing. His influence melted and spread far beyond the sexual heat of his runway." And yet, equally important and influential as Versace's creativity was his craftsmanship. As Turner puts it, "if Versace had been merely a clever stylist, a whiz with fancy buttons and bows, he could not have conquered the world of fashion. The surface

Versace Gives Back

Through the ups and downs in the House of Versace's fortunes, one thing that has remained constant is the Versace siblings' contributions to charities and to their communities. Early and often in his career, Gianni Versace got involved in a number of charitable organizations, most notably Elton John's AIDS Foundation. During her time at the helm of the company, Donatella has donated time, money, and her own celebrity to various causes. In 2005, for example, she helped the Breast Health Institute launch its first real ad campaign and hosted charity events for the organization at the London Versace store.

When an earthquake hit Italy's Abruzzo region in April 2009, Donatella joined others in the fashion industry to design special Coke Light bottles for sale at an auction, with all the money going to support victims of the quake.

The siblings' hometown of Reggio di Calabria has benefited from the Versaces' rise to prominence as well, particularly after Santo was elected to Italy's Parliament in 2008. Luisa Zargani of *WWD* wrote: "Versaces' fame is undoubtedly attracting the media to Calabria, which, located across from Sicily, has always lagged behind in terms of tourism and entertainment. Giusva Branca, editor in chief of online newspaper *Strill*, calls it the 'Versace effect,' noting how the candidate should be able to give credibility to the region."

detailing may have caught the eye, but it was the silhouette that sold the dress."

That creativity and craftsmanship were both just means to an end, however. In both Versace's and Donatella's view, fashion is most important as an expression of individuality and freedom. This has been their message since the beginning of the House of Versace, and it is their most enduring legacy.

THE FUTURE OF VERSACE

As the House of Versace looks toward the future, it faces many of the same challenges as other luxury companies: a global economy still struggling to recover, corresponding weak sales for luxury goods, and a need to define—or redefine—its identity in an uncertain market. Whatever direction the company takes, it appears that Allegra will have a greater voice in deciding it. Ball writes, "In early 2009, Allegra began spending more time in Milan and took up a desk in her mother's atelier." According to Ball, Allegra was involved in the decision that Giancarlo Di Risio needed to go. As the owner of 50 percent of the company, she holds the power to make decisions on her own and outvote Donatella and Santo. So far, however, there have been no signs of strife between her and her mother or uncle.

As the Versaces continue their restructuring and strive to win over consumers, Christopher Kane's work on Versus could show one way forward by serving as a model for bringing in new designers to give Versace labels a fresh look. The collaboration has worked particularly well with Kane, whose own design sense is in line with Donatella's original work on Versus. The *New York Times*'s Horyn wrote: "For those who remember Versus of the early '90s, . . . Mr. Kane's free approach seems just right. Though colorful and sexy, Versus had a strong graphic element with a hip English edge."

Many top designers bring in young talent and take credit for their work, but Donatella has been open about Kane's role in Versus. "It's more believable to young customers to know that Christopher is involved. And being in a company like Versace gives him more relevance," she told Horyn. This attitude could help the house land top young designers looking to make a name for themselves.

While Donatella is reaching out to young customers, she is also keeping Versace's focus on luxury. In May 2010, the company announced a new touch-screen phone, the Versace Unique, starting at $6,900 and getting up as high as $18,800, depending upon the handset exterior. According to Courtney Colavita of *Daily*

Gianni Versace's legacy lives on in the Versace company and in its signature looks. Despite the unpredictability of the fashion industry, Donatella and the rest of the family are committed to creating sexy, glamorous clothes.

News Record, "[K]eeping the brand a thriving luxury company will become [Donatella's] legacy. 'It's been a lot of work to get here and it's even more difficult to maintain it,' says Versace, 'but I'm going to give it everything.'"

For Donatella, giving it everything will include, as it always has, keeping Versace product offerings up to date while staying true to the company's heritage. One of her strengths is having her brother, Santo, and now her daughter, Allegra, to help share the burden of guiding the company forward. Miller of *Second City Style* wrote: "Donatella and her daughter Allegra have adapted the House to the 21st Century with a somewhat softer, more modern, organic sensuality that's just right for today. The Versace name has been consistently recognized for its defiant originality and breakthrough designs: qualities that will continue to inspire for generations to come." The House of Versace and the fashion industry in general are fighting many uphill battles, but in the face of much adversity and even tragedy, Donatella has proved herself a survivor.

Chronology

1946   DECEMBER 2 Gianni Versace born in Reggio di Calabria, Italy.

1955   MAY 2 Donatella Versace born in Reggio di Calabria, Italy.

1978   Gianni Versace presents his first collection under the Versace name.

1982   Gianni Versace introduces Oroton, his patented metal-mesh material.

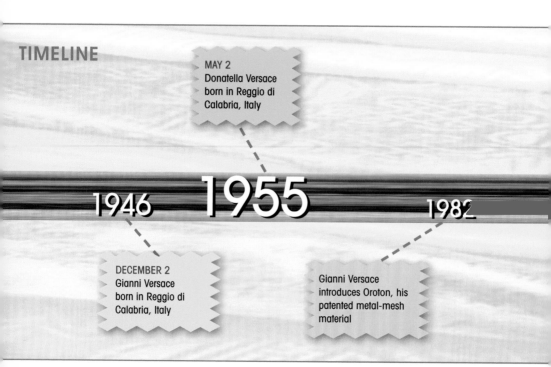

TIMELINE

MAY 2
Donatella Versace
born in Reggio di
Calabria, Italy

1946   **1955**   1982

DECEMBER 2
Gianni Versace
born in Reggio di
Calabria, Italy

Gianni Versace
introduces Oroton, his
patented metal-mesh
material

1991	Gianni Versace wins the final of his four L'Occhio d'Oro awards for the season's best designer.
1994	Elizabeth Hurley wears the "safety-pin dress," one of the most famous red-carpet gowns ever.
1997	Gianni Versace killed in Miami Beach; Donatella becomes head designer.
2004	Allegra Versace Beck turns 18 and inherits Gianni Versace's 50 percent share of the company.
2007	Gianni Versace and Donatella receive plaques on Hollywood's Rodeo Drive Walk of Style.
2009	Company cuts jobs and starts restructuring plan to return to profitability by 2011.

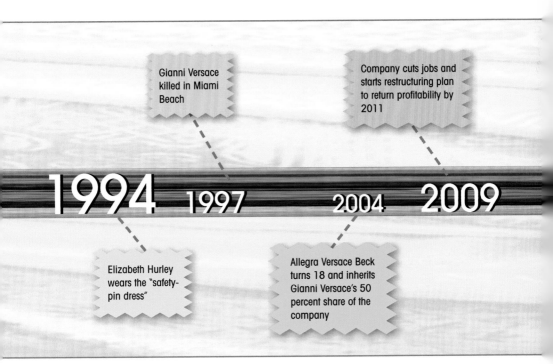

Glossary

atelier   The workshop or studio of an artist, artisan, or designer.

bias cut   Cutting fabric diagonally across the grain, causing a fluid flowing of the material over the body.

bodice   The upper section of a dress or shirt that covers the bust and the torso.

epaulet   An ornamental shoulder accessory on (mainly military officer) uniforms.

haute couture   High fashion; the pinnacle of fashion design and creation.

hem   The bottom edge of a garment or part of a garment sewn to cover the raw edge.

neo-Baroque   A term for extravagant and elaborate ornamentation applied to art, music, architecture, and fashion.

Oroton   A flowing metal-mesh fabric with overlapping rings, patented by Gianni Versace.

prêt-à-porter   Ready-to-wear clothing, factory made and in standard sizes, as opposed to custom-made clothing.

sartorial   Relating to clothing or clothes making.

voile   A lightweight fabric of wool, silk, rayon, or cotton constructed in plain weave.

Bibliography

BOOKS

Ball, Deborah. *House of Versace.* New York: Crown Publishers, 2010.

Buss, Chiara, Valerie Mendes, and Claire Wilcox. *The Art and Craft of Gianni Versace.* London: V&A Publications, 2002.

Calabrese, Omar, and Gianni Versace. *Versace Signatures.* New York: Abbeville Press Publishers, 1992.

Gastel, Minnie. *The Versace Legend.* Milan, Italy: Baldini Castoldi Dalai, 2008.

Turner, Lowri. *Gianni Versace: Fashion's Last Emperor.* London: Essential in association with Chameleon Books, 1997.

Versace, Gianni. *The Art of Being You.* New York: Abbeville Press Publishers, 1997.

INTERNET SOURCES

Bellafante, Ginia, Jordan Bonfante, Cathy Booth, and Georgia Harbison "Gianni Versace: La Dolce Vita." *Time* (July 28, 1997). Available online. URL: http://www.time.com/time/magazine/article/0,9171,986749,00. html. Downloaded on February 9, 2010.

Frankel, Susannah. "Donatella Versace: Prima Donna." *Independent* (September 12, 2006). Available online. URL: http://www. independent.co.uk/news/people/profiles/donatella-versace- prima-donna-415663.html. Downloaded on February 6, 2010.

Goldstein, Lauren. "Armani Mania: Happy Twenty-Fifth." *Time Europe* (December 18, 2000). Available online. URL: http://www.time.com/ time/europe/magazine/2000/1218/armani.html. Downloaded on April 25, 2010.

Greenwald, John. "Will the Versace Fashion Empire Survive?" *Time* (July 28, 1997). Available online. URL: http://www.time.com/time/

magazine/article/0,9171,986754,00.html. Downloaded on February 9, 2010.

Healy, Orla. "Fall of the House of Versace." *Independent* (Ireland) (January 26, 2003). Available online. URL: http://www.independent. ie/unsorted/features/fall-of-the-house-of-versace-488175.html. Downloaded on April 27, 2010.

Horyn, Cathy. "Pretty in Python, Hot in Pastels." *New York Times* (October 4, 2004). Available online. URL: http://www.nytimes.com/2004/10/04/ fashion/04DRES.html. Downloaded on April 29, 2010.

Horyn, Cathy. "The Murder on Ocean Drive." *New York Times* (July 19, 2007). Available online. URL: http://www.nytimes.com/2007/07/19/ fashion/19VERSACE.html. Downloaded on February 2, 2010.

Horyn, Cathy. "Versace and Kane: An Odd Mix That Works." *New York Times* (May 20, 2010). Available online. URL: http://runway.blogs. nytimes.com/2010/05/20/versace-and-kane-an-odd-mix-that-works/. Downloaded on May 31, 2010.

Horyn, Cathy. "Versace and Missoni: Innovation in a Familiar Vein." *New York Times* (February 27, 2006). Available online. URL: http:// www.nytimes.com/2006/02/27/fashion/shows/27FASH.html. Downloaded on February 2, 2010.

Howarth, Peter. "Prima Dona." *Observer* (March 11, 2007). Available online. URL: http://www.guardian.co.uk/lifeandstyle/2007/mar/11/ fashion.features. Downloaded on February 6, 2010.

Khan, Urmee. "Liz Hurley 'Safety Pin' Dress Voted the Greatest Dress." *Telegraph UK* (October 9, 2008). Available online. URL: http:// www.telegraph.co.uk/news/newstopics/celebritynews/3167702/ Liz-Hurley-safety-pin-dress-voted-the-greatest-dress.html. Downloaded on February 17, 2010.

Koda, Harold, and Richard Martin. "Haute Couture," in *Heilbrunn Timeline of Art History*. New York: The Metropolitan Museum of Art, 2000–. Available online. URL: http://www.metmuseum.org/ toah/hd/haut/hd_haut.htm. Downloaded on March 7, 2010.

Krick, Jessa. "Charles Frederick Worth (1826–1895) and the House of Worth," in *Heilbrunn Timeline of Art History*. New York: The Metropolitan Museum of Art, 2000–. Available online. URL: http:// www.metmuseum.org/toah/hd/wrth/hd_wrth.htm. Downloaded on March 7, 2010.

Lacayo, Richard. "Tagged for Murder." *Time* (July 28, 1997). Available online. URL: http://www.time.com/time/magazine/article/0,9171,986747,00. html. Downloaded on February 9, 2010.

Levy, Ariel. "Summer for the Sun Queen." *New York* (August 20, 2006). Available online. URL: http://nymag.com/fashion/06/fall/19388/. Downloaded April 28, 2010.

Menkes, Suzy. "Back to the Future." *New York Times* (January 18, 2010). Available online. URL: http://www.nytimes.com/2010/01/19/fashion/ 19iht-rversace.html. Downloaded on February 2, 2010.

Menkes, Suzy. "Donatella in Wonderland." *New York Times* (September 26, 2009). Available online. URL: http://www.nytimes.com/2009/09/26/ fashion/26iht-rversace.html. Downloaded on May 5, 2010.

Menkes, Suzy. "Versus, Revived." *New York Times* (September 27, 2009). Available online. URL: http://www.nytimes.com/2009/09/28/fashion/ 28iht-rvers.html. Downloaded on February 2, 2010.

Miller, Stephanie. "Va-Va Voom Versace!" *Second City Style.* Available online. URL: http://www.secondcitystyle.com/node/427. Downloaded on March 12, 2010.

Morris, Bernadine. "Saint Laurent Deals His Strong Suit: Easy Separates." *New York Times* (January 26, 1989). Available online. URL: http:// www.nytimes.com/1989/01/26/garden/saint-laurant-deals-his- strong-suit-easy-separates.html. Downloaded on April 8, 2010.

Morris, Bernadine. "In Paris, Magic of Lacroix and Versace." *New York Times* (January 23, 1990). Available online. URL: http://www.nytimes. com/1990/01/23/style/in-paris-magic-of-lacroix-and-versace.html. Downloaded on April 8, 2010.

Peyser, Marc. "Gianni's World." *Newsweek* (July 28, 1997). Available online. URL: http://www.newsweek.com/id/97971. Downloaded on February 13, 2010.

Trebay, Guy. "Why She's the No. 1 Target in the Glamour Business." *New York Times* (February 27, 2006). Available online. URL: http:// www.nytimes.com/2006/02/27/fashion/shows/27DIARY.html. Downloaded on February 5, 2010.

NEWSPAPER AND MAGAZINE ARTICLES

"Bravo Donatella!" *WWD* (October 10, 1997): 1.

"The Cowboy Rides Again: Gianni Versace." *WWD* (March 12, 1992): 1.

"Curves and Waves." *WWD* (October 4, 2001): 6.

"Donatella Divines a New Versace." *WWD* (November 15, 2006): 6B.

"Donatella Gets Personal." *WWD* (October 11, 2004): 18.

"Donatella's New Day: 'Stronger' than Ever as Business Revamps." *WWD* (October 8, 2004): 1.

"Fire and Ice." *WWD* (October 12, 1998): 8.

"Gianni Versace to Present First Couture Collection." *WWD* (December 2, 1988): 15.

"Gianni vs. Giorgio: Is Fashion Dead?" *WWD* (September 11, 1996): 2.

"Hot Stuff." *WWD* (September 28, 2009): 6.

"In Their Own Fashion." *WWD* (October 4, 2004): 6.

"Michael Jackson Selects Versace." *Daily News Record* (June 5, 1991): 3.

"Paris Couture Toujours Glam." *WWD* (July 20, 1998): 6.

"Paris Opens with Dazzle." *WWD* (January 22, 1990): 6.

"Versace Cuts Loss in First Half." *WWD* (September 14, 2005): 6.

"Versace: High Technology." *Daily News Record* (January 19, 1983): 6.

"Versace Launches V2, Women's Diffusion Line." *WWD* (October 10, 1996): 2.

"Versace Loss Hits $32.6 Million in a Year." *Daily News Record* (July 12, 2004): 6.

"Versace Rocks Pitti Uomo; Million-dollar Extravaganza Mixes Ballet and Fashion Glitz." *Daily News Record* (June 27, 1997): COV.

"Versace's Latest Plan: U.S., Accessories Keys to Breaking Even in '07." *WWD* (May 27, 2005): 1.

"When Gianni Met Karl. . . ." *Harper's Bazaar* (October 1993): 61.

Alhadeff, Gini. "Versace's Home Style." *Architectural Digest* (February 1995): 54.

Anderson, Susan Heller. "Chronicle." *New York Times* (January 11, 1991): B4.

Barr, Elizabeth. "Signatures Has Versace Written All Over It." *Daily News Record* (November 9, 1992): 2.

Barry, John, Amy Driscoll, and Bruce Taylor Seeman. "Two Roads to a Fatal Encounter; Party Animal Turns Predator." *Miami Herald* (July 20, 1997): 1A.

Beckett, Kathleen. "Versace Rocks On." *Harper's Bazaar* (November 1992): 168.

Brubach, Holly. "The Sympathy Vote." *New York Times* (August 10, 1997): 643.

Carlsen, Peter. "Gianni Versace: Disciplined Negligence." *GQ* (August 1979): 131.

Carpenter, John, and Phillip J. O'Connor. "Fugitive's Mom Prays for Son; Miglins Deny Knowing Cunanan." *Chicago Sun Times* (May 12, 1997): 1.

Colavita, Courtney. "Family Star." *Daily News Record* (February 5, 2007): 38.

Collins, Lauren. "Mondo Donatella." *The New Yorker* (September 24, 2007): 158.

Colon, Yves, Rick Jervis, and Andres Viglucci. "Stylish Life, Brutal Death: Versace Added Flair, Fame to Beach." *Miami Herald* (July 16, 1997): 1A.

Edelson, Sharon. "Light and Luxe for Versace on Fifth Ave." *WWD* (February 7, 2006): 16.

Foley, Bridget. "Donatella Divines a New Versace." *WWD* (November 15, 2006): 6B.

Forden, Sara Gay. "Versace to Bejart: Fashion to Marry Dance at Pitti Uomo." *Daily News Record* (June 20, 1997): 26.

Furnish, David. "Donatella Versace." *Interview* (April 1996): 56.

Gandee, Charles. "Versace's Castle in the Sand." *Vogue* (December 1994): 290.

Heller, Zoe. "Survivor." *Harper's Bazaar* (August 2000): 182.

Hirshey, Gerri. "Go, Gianni, Go: Designer Gianni Versace Turns His Muse Loose in Miami." *GQ* (May 1993): 63.

Hochswender, Woody. "European Report: Fashion; Milan." *New York Times* (December 15, 1991): 680.

Horyn, Cathy. "A Crisis That's Bigger than Any Handbag." *New York Times* (September 27, 2008): B5.

Horyn, Cathy. "La Bella Donatella." *Vanity Fair* (June 1997): 156.

Ilari, Alessandra, Amanda Kaiser, and Luisa Zargani. "Versace Rumors Swirl over Potential Partners to Aid Balance Sheet." *WWD* (October 27, 2003): 1.

Ilari, Alessandra. "Versace's New Strategy: Eyes 25% Cut in Staff, Return to Black in 2011." *WWD* (October 29, 2009): 1.

Kravitz, Lenny. "Donatella Versace." *Interview* (June–July 2009): 94.

Lee, Andrea. "The Emperor of Dreams." *The New Yorker* (July 28, 1997): 42.

Levine, Joshua. "The Ivory Control Tower." *Forbes* (November 23, 1992): 180.

Merzer, Martin. "Two Roads to a Fatal Encounter; Lives Converge." *Miami Herald* (July 20, 1997): 1A.

Morris, Bernadine. "In Lacroix's Hands, Couture Still Dazzles." *New York Times* (January 26, 1993): B7.

Morris, Bernadine. "In Versace Shop, Theater Lives." *New York Times* (April 24, 1990): B7.

Morris, Bernadine. "Letting Leather Steal the Show." *New York Times* (March 13, 1992): A20.

Mower, Sarah. "Versace Classico." *Harper's Bazaar* (April 1995): 186.

Neill, Michael. "Italy's Gianni Versace Puts Metal Dresses and Miami Vice into Fashion's Grand Design." *People Weekly* (October 20, 1986): 79.

Peres, Daniel. "Donetella de Paris." *WWD* (July 16, 1998): 4.

Ram, Archana. "The Best Style: 1990–2010." *Entertainment Weekly* (March 5, 2010): 60.

Raper, Sarah. "Haute Hype." *WWD* (July 7, 1997): 7.

Rubenstein, Hal. "Gianni Versace." *Interview* (November 1992): 122.

Schiff, Stephen. "Lunch with Mr. Armani, Tea with Mr. Versace, Dinner with Mr. Valentino." *New Yorker* (November 7, 1994): 196.

Schiro, Anne-Marie. "In Milan, a State of Unease on the Runway." *New York Times* (October 13, 1998): B12.

Servin, James. "Chic or Cruel?" *New York Times* (November 1, 1992): 91.

Singer, Sally, and Norman Jean Roy. "Coming Clean." *Vogue* (May 2005): 254.

Sischy, Ingrid. "Style Is Not a Pain in the Neck." *Interview* (June 1995): 58.

Spindler, Amy M. "Another Versace in the Limelight." *New York Times* (March 28, 1996): C10.

Spindler, Amy M. "Gianni Versace, 50, the Designer Who Infused Fashion with Life and Art." *New York Times* (July 16, 1997): A14.

Spindler, Amy M. "In Milan, the Versace Drama Continues." *New York Times* (October 7, 1997): A24.

Spindler, Amy M. "New Word in Couture: Fun." *New York Times* (July 9, 1997): C9.

Spindler, Amy M. "Souls Shine Through." *New York Times* (October 10, 1995): B7.

Spindler, Amy M. "Versace: Clean and Mean for Fall." *New York Times* (March 8, 1995): C10.

Spindler, Amy M. "A Versace Looks Ahead, Through Tears." *New York Times* (October 10, 1997): B7.

Steinhauer, Jennifer. "Unlike Other Fashion Houses, Versace Should Survive Its Founder." *New York Times* (July 19, 1997): 131.

Thomas, Dana. "The Donatella Style." *Newsweek International* (March 8, 1999): 56.

Thomas, Dana. "Fashion Disaster." *Newsweek* (November 16, 2009): 52.

Trebay, Guy. "Restructuring Luxury at Versace." *New York Times* (November 5, 2009): E1.

Van Lenten, Barry. "Gianni's American Dream." *WWD* (April 10, 1995): 13.

White, Constance C.R. "A 2D Versace in the Spotlight." *New York Times* (October 30, 1995): B7.

Zargani, Luisa. "Exhibition Captures Versace, Avedon Connection." *WWD* (February 14, 2008): 18.

Zargani, Luisa. "Santo Versace: From Finery to Freedom Party." *WWD* (April 8, 2008): 7.

Zargani, Luisa. "Versace Profits Drop 30.7% in '08." *WWD* (March 30, 2009): 2.

Further Resources

BOOKS

Ball, Deborah. *House of Versace.* New York: Crown Publishers, 2010.

Buss, Chiara, Valerie Mendes, and Claire Wilcox. *The Art and Craft of Gianni Versace.* London: V&A Publications, 2002.

Farrell-Beck, Jane, and Jean Parsons. *20th Century Dress in the United States.* New York: Fairchild Books & Visuals, 2007.

Jones, Terry, and Susie Rushton. *Fashion Now 2.* Cologne, Germany: Taschen, 2008.

Molho, Renata. *Being Armani: A Biography.* Milan: Baldini Castoldi Dalai Editore Inc., 2008.

Steele, Valerie. *Fashion: Italian Style.* New Haven: Yale University Press, 2003.

WEB SITES

Versace corporate site.
URL: http://www.versace.com

"Donatella & Allegra," *Harper's Bazaar.*
URL: http://www.harpersbazaar.com/magazine/feature-articles/donatella-allegra-versace-0307

"Haute Couture," *Heilbrunn Timeline of Art History.*
URL: http://www.metmuseum.org/toah/hd/haut/hd_haut.htm.

Picture Credits

Index

About the Author

DANIEL K. DAVIS lives in San Francisco with his wife, Carrie, and their son, Cai. He graduated from the University of California, Berkeley, with a bachelor's degree in English.